THE WRECK OF THE FATHERSHIP

W.N. [Bill] Herbert is a highly versatile poet who writes both in English and Scots. Born in Dundee, he established his reputation with two English/Scots collections from Bloodaxe, *Forked Tongue* (1994) and *Cabaret McGonagall* (1996). These were followed by *The Laurelude* (1998), *The Big Bumper Book of Troy* (2002), *Bad Shaman Blues* (2006), *Omnesia* (2013) and *The Wreck of the Fathership* (2020). He has also published a critical study, *To Circumjack MacDiarmid* (OUP, 1992), drawn from his PhD research. His practical guide *Writing Poetry* was published by Routledge in 2010. He co-edited *Strong Words: modern poets on modern poetry* (Bloodaxe Books, 2000) with Matthew Hollis, and *Jade Ladder: Contemporary Chinese Poetry* (Bloodaxe Books, 2012) with Yang Lian. Bill Herbert is Professor of Poetry and Creative Writing at Newcastle University and lives in a lighthouse overlooking the River Tyne at North Shields. He was Dundee's inaugural Makar from 2013 to 2018.

Twice shortlisted for the T.S. Eliot Prize, his collections have also been shortlisted for the Forward Prize, McVities Prize, Saltire Awards and Saltire Society Scottish Book of the Year Award. Four are Poetry Book Society Recommendations. In 2014 he was awarded a Cholmondeley Prize for his poetry, and an honorary doctorate from Dundee University. In 2015 he became a Fellow of the Royal Society of Literature.

THE WRECK OF THE FATHERSHIP

W.N. HERBERT

BLOODAXE BOOKS

Copyright © W.N. Herbert 2020

ISBN: 978 1 78037 524 3

First published 2020 by
Bloodaxe Books Ltd,
Eastburn,
South Park,
Hexham,
Northumberland NE46 1BS.

www.bloodaxebooks.com
For further information about Bloodaxe titles
please visit our website and join our mailing list
or write to the above address for a catalogue.

Supported by
**ARTS COUNCIL
ENGLAND**

Cover design: Neil Astley & Pamela Robertson-Pearce.

Printed in Great Britain by Bell & Bain Limited, Glasgow, Scotland, on
acid-free paper sourced from mills with FSC chain of custody certification.

For my Father

(William Powrie Herbert, 1937-2014)

The souls of the dead are the spirit of language:
you hear them alight inside that spoken thought.

DENISE RILEY

ACKNOWLEDGEMENTS

Thanks are due to the following magazines, anthologies and other publications: *Dostoyevsky Wannabe Cities: Dundee, Hargeysa Breeze, The National, Natural Light II, New Humanist, Perverse, Ploughshares, Poetry London, Seagate III* and *The Voyage Out*.

'*Address to the Dundee V&A*' was broadcast on *STV News* in September 2018. 'Tyne Valley Section' appeared as part of a collaboration with Sean O'Brien, 'In These Waters' for BALTIC, 2018. 'Mastercannibal' appeared in *Scotia Extremis*, edited by Andy Jackson and Brian Johnstone (Luath, 2018). 'The Muriels' appeared in *Spark: Poetry and Art Inspired by the Novels of Muriel Spark*, ed. Rob A. Mackenzie and Louise Peterkin (Blue Diode, 2018). 'The Nightfishing' appeared in *The Caught Habits of Language: An Entertainment for W.S. Graham*, ed. Rachael Boast, Andy Ching, Nathan Hamilton (Donut Press, 2018). 'The Nine Trades Welcome You to the City of Refuge' was commissioned for *Festival of the Future City*, ed. Andre Kell and Melanie Kelly (Bristol Cultural Development Partnership, 2015). 'Whose English Is It Anyway?' was commissioned by *The Verb* as part of the BBC Free Thinking Festival, September 2014. 'Mother Goo' was written for *Slanted: Twelve Poems for Christmas*, ed. Helen Ivory and Kate Birch (Ink Sweat & Tears, 2013). 'The Lost Poem' and 'North of the Book' were commissioned by Newcastle Centre for the Literary Arts; the latter appeared in *Shadow Script*, ed. Colette Bryce (NCLA, 2013), and was broadcast on BBC Radio 4.

Dundee Doldrums is a continuation of a sequence of poems begun in the pamphlet *Dundee Doldrums* (Galliard, Edinburgh, 1991), four of which were included in *Forked Tongue* (Bloodaxe Books, 1994).

I should also like to thank the School of English at Newcastle University for their continuing support, and Dundee University for creating the post of Dundee Makar, which it has been an honour to hold, as well as for the honorary degree they conferred on me in 2014.

CONTENTS

ALGOS

JESUS MARY AND JETSAM 1

THE WRECK OF THE FATHERSHIP

Fathership Glosa

> I had to come
> I had no say
> I was not here
> I could not stay

Your death poem, Dad, was premature:
through the haemangioma's coils
Mr O'Malley of the Mater
made katabasis of your entrails,
stitched you on time with sure sutures.
That your labyrinth's core might be your tomb
turned you half-Kirkton minotaur,
half-samurai somehow Dundee-born –
so your scribbled *jisei* was begun
       I had to come

Near sixty I forget what you knew
at sixteen: why you were running down
new waterpipes' long darkness to
Lintrathen. Then that paper round's
small epic – you still held its clew:
each close and every name in a maze
of tenements. You brought our town
cleanliness, yet at sea you'd sound
the propeller's keel-crawl shaft and gauge
       I had no say

Twenty years after your revival,
no poet still you've made it stick,
that death quatrain that will not die, while,
no engineer, mine will not tick,
this knock-off time-piece of your psyche
fails now what was you jams, a gear
that can't be wound, though from its wreck
your able-bodied rhetoric
sums up our brief and vital fear
       I was not here

'Gless Erse,' your sister called you – true
cruel-to-be-tender Herbert wit,
referring to that Worthy fool
of Dundee lore who could not sit
for fear of shattering his cul.
Just so you had to be away
at once from stuckness: first to sea;
then down the pub; and now leave me
aboard days' bottled barque for always:
          I could not stay

GOOD MAKAR

When my father died
we put him in the ground
When my father died
it was like a whole library
burned down.

LAURIE ANDERSON

Cuttlefish Bone

White shoehorn to the sea's boot,
spectacle case for the ghosts of eyes,
palate within tides' mouth:

all tissue worn away by water's gnaw,
your flesh was sea's to wede awa, as
you're being borne to land attests,

beached and bleached like the breast
of a seabird downed by storm, wings
folded by the grave waves, beak

turned into the shingle; symbol
of being's forgetfulness, that
it would leave you anywhere

and here, as though an anamorph
I could angle to see my own skull by,
mirror of bone – the thinking hand

that held you, boneless to
its fingertips except for you,
long since let go.

Nightfishing

(after Picasso)

> Very gently struck
> The quay night bell
>> W.S. GRAHAM

1

Way down in the warm blue crevasse
of night its fishing commences as
the boat of millions of fingernails drags
across a blackboard-winged bay.

Across the painted harbour at Antibes
we see a painting of Broughty Castle
in which the back of my father's head is
looking back at me covered in seaweed.

He was the rock from which I threw all
those nude tarnished spoons like the stars
of heaven landing as soft shoe crabs, or as
a spattered dress on the Phibbie Pier.

Olga the cross-legged ballerina and
Dora-Thérèse of the Arse-parked Bicycle
look on. Two scoops of testicle
are lifted to a scalene tongue.

2

Like a yoyo the old apocalypse comet
twirls from Mrs Picasso's celadon sleeve,
and is shot over the green igloo cheek
of the harbour wall by our common

lust to see through the language, that *origine
du monde* Venn-diagrammed between
night's labia of dreaming and grief –
did you hearsee or saw it beneath

the torches like twists of lemon sweets, with
a fork for our gladiatorial silverware? The quartz
fish records your squint like a stubbled general
under its thumbed-back lid of waters;

it is a word deloused of mere speakers,
naked amid this kelp of ekphrasis,
its etymology more like sleep itself, which
our sloth-faced fisher in the stripy T-shirt

of yamming what he yam
has a stab at. Nightmatters prefer their own
spectrum of purples and olive green, but get
crumpled newspapers of anatomies

in the globe of bluejeans and spinepelt, alpha
boat of wet elbows, nostrils leaving
their own faces in a flare of want,
kill glimpsed through displacement

of krill. Dora's face is slapped by the paint
brush into a doormat of distress above
Thérèse's breasts and genitals brush
stroked into a pyramid dress and a prone heart.

The reticule of light is folded over
the bow as we lose hold on the heat of
the hand of what those we loved knew,
so improvise the retention of ice.

   3
From the porthole rubbed in
the restaurant window in the colour
less predawn my father sips his sage tea,
preparing for this ferry that will slip

beneath the vault of ice as though between
a whale's blue ribs back to that cavewall
of tattoos, back when the word
and the mark and our skin were one.

18

Beneath the tongues of all the fishes,
the pierwomen claim, is the real name
of his port of call; in one of their bellies,
reply the fishspearers, rests his wedding ring.

Beneath the whalefish eye of a raw sun,
the singing that does not know
it is song; within its lyrics without words,
the word to be that must have loved us.

Broughty Ferry Beach: a renga

A half a mile strip
of small whitish mussel shells
on the sandy beach

A mother of pearly way
I walk east to Monifieth.

The empty crab shell
lies upended in the surf
and shouts at the sky.

The clouds' lead lid can't linger,
but still takes all day to shift.

A sparrow, grabbing
a gull's feather, flies off with
long white moustaches.

Two ducks tuck away their heads
like green slippers on the lawn.

Rain flicks pearls upon
the pane, same size as the gulls
bobbing in the Tay.

The children are not afraid of the rain.
The rain is not afraid of the children.

Between the showers
tarmac in the railings' shade
has no time to dry

and casts a double shadow
of light's absence and black wet.

In the evening
a heron's silhouette stalks
flukes in the shallows

Swans have no airs: they settle
on the mud and go to sleep.

Haar billowing up
the river in clouds, burning
away as it goes,

veiling and unveiling Fife.
One window catching sunlight

bores through it. One bird-
like shape between, dragoman
of light, floats, shining.

Curlews on their reedy stilts:
hummingbirds at Tay's flower.

Dogs don't know or care
they've never been taught to swim
which is why they can.

White waves; white gulls, while, between,
swans make numbers with their necks.

Tay reverts to gray
like a painter whose palette
is already mixed,

flicking ink flecks in mid-stream,
fine lines drawing in to shore.

The guardrail's shadow
zigzags down its steps into
the sea, sawtooth, like

stonework on a Norman arch
invading the shoreline's curve.

Two swans taking flight
shift feathers from sheltered grey
to morning's bright blaze.

Geese print their one letter
alphabet out across the sky.

A wee girl holds up
two slices of brown bread to
hundreds of seagulls

who descend on her as though
she were a human sandwich.

On Balgay Hill

Cross thi bonny blue brig o Balgay
atween thi livin and thi deid:
here thi Mills observes the Milky Way,
there they eh thi Styx insteid.

Gilfillan bides tae greet ye there,
His obelisk amang thi pines:
Ayont, the stanes ascend thi brae
in braithless zigzag lines.

Ask him as a Virgil whaur
thi graves o wir associates leh.
thi banes o the deid recede lyk stars
intil thi hill's mirk skeh.

Thae constellations under gress
lose myths at whilk he cannae guess.

brig: bridge; *eh*: eye; *bides*: stays, waits; *ayont*: beyond; *mirk*: dark; *whilk*: which.

Blackness Caganer

Billy Monachie – Eh tell nae leh
shat his pants as thi Queen drove beh.

Kids aa lined thi auld Perth Road
and Billy squaatted like a toad:

Blackness Skail's ain cacky knave
as the black car passed wi a gracious wave

tae the bairns wha lauched and grat and howled,
and thi republican in Billy's bowels.

Later, telt tae scrieve a poem,
Eh thocht o thi Queen and her wee broon gnome.

And iver sin syne a limousine
huz fur me a fecal gleam.

caganer: figurine depicted in the act of defecation [Catalan]; *skail*: school; *scrieve*: write.

Ghost Bowling

In the darkness of December in Orchar Park,
beyond the wrought iron fence
I can't quite see, behind the high black hedge
I can barely make out, a light is on.

Night after night Dad drives me past,
and out of the corner of my eye, beneath
the clouded or cloudless sky,
edged with or obliterated without

its moon, filling or emptying;
beneath and before the leafless black canopies
of trees that flank the railway track,
its unseen continuous passing-throughness,

the verandah of the bowling club is lit.
Four wooden pillars stand, thin as noodles
in the yellow soup. They are the edges
of bright, floating oblongs, and from them

light fans across that portion of lawn
I can glimpse through the gap in the hedge.
This composition is all dark frame, cupping
the small shapes light likes to make

to make night guilty. It suggests but does not allow
the dead knock of bowl against bowl,
the disembodied hand releasing their curve.
I pass by the bowling club's small rule

amid a great freedom
that the darkness doesn't share.

The Dundee Eve

When Nick learnt Eve wiz fae Dundee
he hud tae cheenge iz lehs:
a diet o fruit diz not agree
wi a lassie raised oan pehs.

'An aippul!' she sais, 'Whit yais is thon?
Hope you're no sayin Eh'm fat?'
'Christ, no!' sais thi Deil. 'Here, hae a cheese scone.'
'Dje hae ony jeely wi that?'

'Thi aippul appears in aa thi best tales,
and ut's aye fur thi bonniest quean;
Atalanta, Snow White, thi Princess o Wales,
or Venus…' 'Eh hear whit ye're sayin!

'Thae weemen aa soond lyk fancy celebs
while Eh huv barely nae airs,
less knickers nor graces – ane o thi plebs:
yir aippul's fur them up thi stairs.'

'You're sonsier, sexier, donsier, deft
and fitter by faur fur this *pomme*!'
'Eh, and Eh must be thi anely wan left –
withoot me ye'll hae nae rom-com.'

'Ye're smerter nor Adam…' 'Waatch whit ye're sayin –
he's hermless till he's hud a think.
He made up a Gode when he bided alane…'
'Eh think Eh could dae wi a drink.'

'A cider fur me frae thi fruit o this tree –
we hud a braw breein last year.'
'Ye've drunk it?' 'Ut beats thon shite herbal tea –
and thi scrumpin wiz meh idea.'

'But hoo did Gode no know ye'd sought
thi kennan o guid fae evil?'
'At nicht we micht, but thi morn we forgot –
an thi details ur thi deevil…'

Nick pleadit wi Gode tae pley thi gemm
if He waantit Adam tae faa
and set him up wi some ither dame
fae onywhaur else at aa.

'Let Adam faa an brak'iz neck,'
thi Deity replehd,
'Wu'll still aa be at Evie's beck…'
And He and Auld Nick seghed.

lehs: lies; *yais*: use; *jeely*: jam; *quean*: young woman; *sonsier*: heartier; *donsier*: more self-possessed;
breein: brewing; *kennan*: knowing; *faa*: fall.

Clouds at Night

Clouds at night like dolphins dream
with half a mind on Hamlet –
they sketch out the cotton monster mouths,
doodle the dough topographies, the Gnome;
pen profiles of noble hounds, the bones
of future skies, far grander than
any hitherto witnessed by lovers on their backs
gasping in the aftermath of a pleasure
that passes, slow as cirrus.

Their water droplet brains cannot be seen
except as sullen rounds, caught in searchlights,
or a boiling chicken soup of lightnings, looked
down upon by night-flights, so
they can abandon all their codes –
decumulate, bring alterity to alto,
be more nimble than nimbus, stray
from the stratus path.
                    They out-flock floccus,
are more tortoise than intortus, less
spineless than vertebratus. Just as
shellfish don't know the colours
inside their shells, we can't see
how nacreous they get: this goes beyond
noctilucence
            into the registers that blinded bats.

It's only at night that we suspect
the world has turned its back on us,
when clouds prepare their sleet of hands,
and mark their sliced bread decks.
They fold themselves into
the rag paper shapes that furniture is not
but fears it will become, the soft alternatives.

We have to let them pulse between lenticular
and lacunar; be fallstreak hole and UFO,
air jellyfish and whirling cosmic pill-stack.
They must transmit to eager insect sects
now hopping on the Moon, ready to begin
Lunar Lent. Message sent.

Tay Nocturne

Atween the streetlichts here i thi Ferry
and a late lowe owre Fife
it's no eneuch tae tell
the silhouettes o the geese, crossin

abune the river i thir hunners
quhilk-quhilkin and skreichin unseen
heidin sooth o November,
sooth o thi v-rods still cut in stanes

i thi daurk lanes and loans
o thi fowk that passed afore thum
ridin north o aathin, west o onywan

thir voices ayont thi hearin o geese
near as they can fleh
tae nae place ava.

lowe: glow; *eneuch*: enough; *v-rods*: Pictish symbols; *loans*: strips of grass; *ava*: at all.

The Road Bridge

On the other side of the clouds
meteorites are scratching the black
to be let out. Down here,

the bracelet of the bridge's lights
is bare of cars for five minutes
in which you can imagine its lanes

empty at the mid-point,
the river rushing below, as though
the opposite of its
                           static tar.

You can put yourself there,
as though no more cars
would ever cross, as though

there would be no dawn, as though
the lights would never go out,
and you'd never see the stars again.

You can live there for a while,
while watching yourself
from a few miles off. You're lying

in the road, just staring up.
You have always been this far away
from your life, this perfectly alone.

The Three Flies

Three Dundee flehs went driftin aff
oan a teatray owre thi Tay –
they thocht they'd flocht tae Fife fur a laugh
on an October day.

Thi waater wiz as blue as Peter,
thi skeh as clear as mince,
thi Storm Fiend hoavert lyk a skeeter,
Tay's cycle switched tae 'Rinse'.

They saw twa swaans black as baleen
fur flehs see in reverse
lyk tapsalteerie submarines
thir periscopes immerse.

They landit oan a sandbank caad
Thi Haufwey Hoose o Tay,
whaur Mona's droonit crew, crab-gnaad,
wi Monck's auld sailors played.

Thir fitbaa wiz a cannonball,
thi gemm wiz lang an slow;
thi three flehs eht a peh, enthralled –
tho why, they didnae know.

Thi furst fleh muttert tae his pal,
'This somehow seems symbolic…'
Thi second said, 'Meh nemm is Baal,
and Eh'm a crapoholic.'

Thi three flehs pushed aff frae thi bank,
and headit fur Tentsmuir;
thi Storm Fiend thru thi grey cloods slank,
anniz motives werr impure.

Afore they passed thi auld Pile Licht,
a gairfish louped thi tray –
'Fuck you!' they bizzed, as aff it whizzed
lyk a sine wave thru thi Tay.

Thi second fleh addressed thi third,
'Dae sic things hae a meanin?'
His brither said, 'When you're a turd,
yir specs will aye need cleanin.'

Afore they clipped thon hangnail beach
or touched thi shore o Fife,
thi Storm Fiend reached, his airm ootstreitched,
while whusslin, 'Sic is life...'

'Please state yir nemms tae thi Abysm,'
he asked as thunner crashed.
'We're Jute n Jam n Journalism,'
Ane answert unabashed.

'We're fleas unto thi Wedderburns,'
sez Twa, as fell waves waashed.
'We're crehd Yestreen, Thi Dey, Thi Morn,'
sez Three in yon stramash.

Thi Storm Fiend steyed his haund, 'Ah yes,'
he seghed, 'whit's in a name?
Eh hae tae catch a damned express...'
and skiffied them back hame.

thocht, flocht: thought, float; *tapsalteerie*: inverted; *eht, peh*: ate, pie; *anniz*: and his; *gairfish*: dolphin; *louped*: leapt; *stramash*: commotion; *skiffied*: throw a flat stone so that it bounces across the water.

Tay Lightning

The lightning isn't here yet.
It doesn't want to strike us,
or so the clouds say
at first.

The river and the princes of the air
are at one
in their momentary deadpan glow:
NOW, and again, NOW.

Thunder takes so long to arrive
it might be another era's,
boiling up from ships'
holds, shifting

in the sands beyond the bar;
boomed from caves still
blinking at
the after-images of saints.

When it comes again
and again, nearer,
I'm never looking at
the colourless

ness of grass and wave:
their true form
concealed from us by the sun
as much as night.

When the lightning arrives
in its chariot of silence
and teeth,
it is a letter standing

between cloud and water;
it is the calligraphy of passing
we cannot read
still thrumming on my eyelids

that flinch as a heron is
released into my head.
I take in the castle,
the harbour and the bridge:

all normal again
as though they were still real.

Beach Terrace

I

The swans glow grey in the night harbour,
that birthing curve where no more boats will beach;
its shingle cups the darkness with both hands.

The swans are no more asleep than streetlamps
across the Tay, the creeping pulse of cars
upon the bridge, or the oilrigs' brilliant ladders,

clambering into a cloud-craft over the Stannergate.
The swans in their dirty ganseys of feathers pace
the tide's deck, restless for their watch's end.

The lights contrive to make an arc, an eyebrow
from west to east, capping the harbour's socket,
Thus opening a dark eye through which Tay stares

into the starlessness – small wonder that the swans
can't sleep, clinging like eyelashes to the shore.

II

Woken by a ghost helicopter at 7 a.m.
hovering overhead and giving our building
the shakes, I come through to the river
still basking in the arrival of light.

Gulls swoop so low I catch the gleam
of their reflection on the nearest wave,
then group into a gaunt cloud of feathers
crested with warmth and buoyed by the wind

off the water. An airplane mimics
the look of the light on their backs and wheels
upriver, receding over the roadbridge to land.

The rooks, a compact of wrack and the shadow
under the pier, point out the shortest distance
into the issuing teeth of the morning blast.

III

Swans in the smirr, the river at full brim,
tide printing with weed's font upon the shore.
Fife almost filtered out by mist's cool scrim
between the grain of wavecrest and cloud smore

that slowly rises like a clam to let
light back: at first, a gesso slaister, lain
across the water like a swan in flight,
its neck extended through departing rain;

then evening turns it milk and mango neon,
and chains and lirks of darkness slide and switch
as though to cut the sun-trail's throat, though no one
seems threatened by Tay's gothic Etch a Sketch.

The swans all clamber out like limber matrons
while one drifts off, as dark as punctuation.

IV

Through some error when I wake up
my father is still dead. Blobs of Tay foam
still move swiftly past on the outgoing tide
and a rainbow's whale rib leans between

some drizzle and Dundee. The fit flee fate
briskly on foot or by bicycle or with dog.
Preening, a swan denies that it has feet, while
the heron is a gaunt tusk by the harbour wall.

That snowball fight in the height of summer
in the heat of dry dock in Hong Kong:
grown men playing with asbestos in the hold

of the *Javanese Princess*, too young,
too early in their century, to know each strike
would take its own sweet decades to be fatal.

V

The occasion of a death, with or without
its auspices – these sounds of an empty room,
how two clocks fake a heartbeat out
of inexactitude; fire's gassy bloom.

How the cord slipped easy between the fingers
launching the body in its final boat.
How you must recount instead of listen,
narrate what you, poor editor, forgot.

The mist blows up the river and comforts us
that what it eats is not digested, pulp,
but there still, still in the unstill, across
the conjectured, trusted waves, the low cloud's gulf.

Tell us – tell yourself – of the ends of endings:
imagining beyonds is beyond mending.

VI

The buildings in the river's reflection of the town
are not the same as the buildings in the town:
its mirror remembers the demolished and the dead,
whose faces pass while you gaze into the waves.

Every ninth wave is a wave that has already crashed;
every nine hundredth raindrop has already fallen;
you are never more than nine miles from your double;
your tears replay the same grief on a nine year cycle.

Believers in eternal life are jealous of Moses
who has enjoyed thousands of years more than them.
The final prophet has nothing left to prophesy.

Divers are sworn not to tell, but beneath the grey
and angry waves, to the astonishment of fish, this life
plays out upside down, and on a nine second delay.

VII

The wind's inventing whiteness again,
in the breaching caps of waves,
an equivalence between paper and gulls,

and the bearing of tide's teeth upon the beach:
its long white snarl. It even tunes
the briskness of women, the engines of dogs.

I lie back and the bay window fills with river,
its frame editing out the shoreline till
I could almost be afloat in fact as in this life.

The wind snores in the chimney's throat,
dreams of becoming visible, a forest
of fingertips without fingers, hands or arms;

it dreams its prints are revealed everywhere,
so it never has to touch everything ever again.

VIII

Why do we think of them at all, the dead,
since they can never come again, except
there is a part which cannot – not accept,
but, somehow, cannot know. And so, instead

we worry at their absence till it seems
to share their likeness, growing older as
they will not, till it almost comes to pass
for them in those sad simulacra, dreams.

Our animal's non-narrative, can't know
the dead are dead, so sees them everywhere:
we're fooled by innocence into despair,
and thus our lost can never be let go.

The continuity we call our days
has caught all dupes and doubles in its maze.

The Continuity

What happens to the surface when you know
how any moment now it might be broken
as this May river is by dolphins' backs?
Five years I've studied Tay's broad palimpsest
high in this rented flat's bay window, watched
their slick backs breach in brilliant morning light
or idle back to sea in evening's stillness;

seen lightning walk the midnight water, Moon
enamel it, Fife streetlights cast their rods
and floats upon it. Watched the swans return
each morning round the rounded pier, as though
they were legations from light's see, or land
with outspread wings announcing, as their feet

create a broken wafer's edge, we are
with and within a continuity.
I've watched the heron watch, its beak a nib,
its eye all-piercing of the shallows by
the harbour – water, prey or shingle, or
the bed on which the Tay can never rest.

Less than a year I'd had here when he died
whose arms these steady piers impersonate,
whose hand my memory still holds, to feel
its warmth pass into mine, and, fading, print
its feel upon the parchment of the palm.
Surfaces are where we suppose ourselves
as creatures who infer that we have depths.

June Dolphin

1

Thi hert loups wi thi gairfish
in uts waatirgaw o spray,
o ee an muscle, licht and air-rush
in mornin oan thi Tay.

Ye needna be a bairnie, or
hae keethin sicht o ocht
tae see whit ithers carena fur
an laive ahint aa thocht.

2

Laive loss ahint as weel,
altho it maun retour:
that loup sees time mishantlet till
an instant is an oor.

Ererniry's aneath us,
it's millt upon thi beach –
we kenna hoo sic ithers keeth us,
nor intae whit we breach.

loups: leaps; *waatirgaw*: rainbow; *ee*: eye; *bairnie*: small child; *keethin sicht*: disturbances
caused by the movements of fish; *ocht*: anything; *laive ahint*: leave behind; *maun retour*: must
return; *mishantlet*: miscalculated; *oor*: hour; *kenna*: know not; *keeth*: perceive.

Kafka Eskimo

One morning Angutii awoke to find he'd been transformed
into Pingu, an ageing plasticine penguin.

After only a few years of gibber and squeak
on children's TV, it appeared
his second career as the porn star 'Dirty Pingu'
had proven unhappily brief.

One morning Angutii awoke to find himself in a yellow canoe
stuffed to the gunnels with the stolen gold
of medieval Dundee, and sinking fast.

Angutii awoke to find two bailiffs
from the City Council battering at his igloo door –
apparently he had not paid his Ice Rates
in two hundred years. It was morning.
A platypus upon the pletty blinked at him.

One morning Angutii awoke, and knew instinctively
that something was wrong.

Angutii awoke before dawn one morning to find himself
eating contaminated canned corned beef with Franklin
and all his maddened men.

Angutii awoke to find he had been transformed
into Ringo, and must shuffle onto the deck
of his flying saucer, park/crashed illegally
on top of the Mills Observatory, on Balgay Hill.

It was still early. Behind him he heard
the start-up programme for Blubberthug the robot walrus;
before him the Lord Provost and
the thirty seven piece City of Discovery Brass Band
awaited his news nervously.

One morning Angutii awoke to feel stubble growing through
his cold claymation cheeks.

Angutii awoke to find he had been transformed
into Michael Marra, and was playing honkytonk
on an ice-floe to a polar bear, who was swigging
from a giant bottle of ersatz cola.

He looked at his hands, still playing in the morning light,
he looked at his hands
and saw they had been turned into fingerless flippers.

One morning Angutii awoke, still in his kayak
but paddling up the River Tay
as though the axle of the world
had somehow in the night been greased with blubber
and had loosened off –

Fife to the left of him, the Law to the right,
everything de-iced and lacking seals.

Rain Habbies

The rain it raineth on the Tay,
turnin silver intae gray,
waashin aa the waves away
    bar seven swans –
its million pockmarks mar the day;
    the heavens yawn.

A man went aff the bridge, they say
evadin aa authority
returnin tae the womb of Tay,
    he crossed the bar:
today, high tide has brocht a stray
    memorial spar.

Blackly in the harbour's sway
the driftwood bobs in drizzle's spray
and slowly, slowly slips away
    bleak as the throat
of a diving bird wha finds the Tay
    withoot a boat.

Burns' Night Impromptu

Here's tae thi deid and here's tae thi livin:
thi former, mind, ur mair forgivin
gin ye pour them oot a gless or seven
            then drink it yersel –
tae luke doon on thi like fae Heaven,
            it maun be hell!

And gin they're in thi ither place
or mellit wi nocht in ooter space,
gee thanks fur this sma interface –
            respite fae dreid.
The Deil recites thi Selkirk Grace
            an bous his heid.

Thi livin like tae flech thir scaurs
and get back tae thir feckless wars,
but fur this meenut, sit indoors
            and share a dram:
Burns kent thi worth o siclike splores
            is fient a damn.

Sae luke intae ilk ither's een
be they thi absent or thi seen,
and ask yirsels: whit diz it mean
            tae be thigither?
The morn's morn is anither scene,
            anither weather.

gin: if; *maun*: must; *mellit wi nocht*: mingled with nothingness; *bous*: bows; *flech*: scratch as
though one had fleas; *siclike splores*: such antics; *fient a damn*: less than nothing; *the morn's
morn*: tomorrow morning.

Bregus

(Cardiff)

The blossom has almost come to this cherry tree
in the Gorsedd Gardens, like its Japanese name
with its too many syllables to my memory. Its buds,
though bursting and unfurling, are unfulfilled
as yet, still as it were in their yesterday, before
the full bloom, though every pore of its
too many arms is stretched upon the cross-less sky.

Yaezakura. Like the one they planted too near
our old house and the garage with my father's
fine engineering tools, rusting in their wooden trays:
shut drawers' laminae peeling too near the hours
I spent growing in all the directions of the clumsy soul,
the years of forcing the you you want to be
when you don't know the air you're growing into.

So too this tree is near enough to an exhibition
of ceramics, its brittle vitrines cradling porcelain,
to allow an association: those broken bowls –
although the name for this escapes me too –
repaired with golden lacquer in the calligraphy
of grief, its language tonal, the monosyllables
of shattering. *Kintsukuroi*. Like fragments

of china in the East Balgillo fields, his death
comes back to me in broken things: that glass
of my grandmother's, painted with thin gold stars;
our blue jug sketched with freshwater shrimp;
the Brown Betty teapot, the lid of which I dropped
down a stairwell, and found nearly all its parts.
And in that cherry tree he felled, very like a truth.

bregus: fragile [Welsh]

Physic

(Dundee Botanic Gardens)

How silently returning to their plant hammam,
its several categories of heat, we recognise
in these nodding silhouettes our otherness
from all planets but our heads.

Ananas lucidus; Bullhorn acacia; Pachystachys lutea

How in birdless exiled orbit they already
almost are, the near insect-free glasshouses
we have placed not in outer but within
a civic space, that we may bring them
atmosphere like humming wings
through the timed adjustment of hatches,
the opening of panes to distanced light.

Keep the Aspidistra lurida flying.

In our longing not to be alone, but in solitary
solidarity with them we gaze, we sketch, we snap,
we defer to let each other pass
back out into the north of the void. We see
how their names and their appearances
have begun to drift apart
in our gravity-free need not to know, only
to know how to know.

Calathea musaica; Poor Knight's Lily; Boweia volubilis

How we are compelled to read
ourselves into their eyeless realm
of sticky frond, bark-spike, and seed-nozzle
till flowers have faces and stalks grow dactylic.

How far into us this ascription intends,
until we can't not see that figure, inked out
in some kink of desert limbs, framed
by some other branches' helpful angles.

Agave Americana 'medio-Picta Alba'

It is from our whole being's habit
that we inherit this glass-chested robot,
green-brained, thought-shaded;
this gathering not feared enough for,
and only apprehended in the tending.

The Angels' Trumpets need not sound

We must take physic from what we do
not know, or knowing cannot name,
or naming do not recognise.
Take physic from the space between
those certainties in which we live
and die as surely as such useful botanics
should supply poultice, tincture, or cure;
from that alleviation knowing or
our wish to know should bring.

Salary

Lately I crave its pinch, nape of sea,
and know I have inherited, carrying
my father's taste into the home

he cannot see me in. What drew them
to salt's excess, our fathers? Yours balancing
the slice of butter on his toast, mine shaking

and shaking, enduring like heat or
hangover, the scolding poured forth
with the cellar's upending, the emptying

into the ghost-half of its
hourglass.
Not

just
the ration,
nor the bowls upon

the mess's tables in the tropics
of his youth, tablets enticing these boys
to eat the ocean they were crossing,

sweat it all back out in engine rooms
of tramp ships, work it out like years
then eat some more, work as time, as tidal.

I turn the clear plastic middle-class mill
dry sleeting into my porridge, and look out
at Tay's accepting of the salt tongue of the sea.

The Swans at Broughty Ferry Beach

Tayport's lights skinkle
like fishscales, send their shafts down;
the Moon's half-engaged.

We've seen this before:
the broad path of cutlery,
the jutting black pier;

granted that it's vast,
that the mind can grasp at miles
of moon-touched water;

that these two swans, by
gliding in the harbour gloom,
make this proximate,

are emissaries –
what's this metaphysics to us
who glance and pass?

We've people to leave
and homes to get to: it is
Saturday night.

And yet we slow down,
we pause to watch the swans move
across the Moon's waves.

It's like we're children
watching the grey men hopping
inside our TV

and realising
just how far away we are
from everything:

from the astronauts,
from the TV, our parents,
even from ourselves.

Perhaps the swans are
a measure, showing how far
away the world is.

Like carpentry tools,
bladeless, their necks for handles,
the swans plane the waves.

Their black, thoughtless eyes,
their wings' absolute stillness:
their indifference

is a match for ours.
The Moon may not pay witness
to us, but they could,

just like we suppose
we would, some day, if obliged,
pause by the river,

observe the moonlight
fill the waves with forks and knives,
and be cut by swans.

Sunday Morning Improv

Tay seems to rush towards the sunlight
as it hits eastern-facing walls and windows
across from Broughty Ferry
and burns the mist off Fife.

Darker waves, rising where currents meet
harbours' contrarinesses,
remember and want to be
the backs of porpoises.

I divide the river by my windows,
eye it near to far, looking for
trout or salmon's random splash,
the recurring swift intent of dolphins' backs.

The white lighthouse where you can't land,
neither tooth nor horn, nonetheless sends
a sharp spike of itself
down into the reflecting water.

Each morning, the fishermen are always
already at the pier's end,
risen and watching and ready,
at their nexus of the nextness.

A cloud-bank comes and cauls the sun,
dulling Tay's sheen,
declaring early's over,
and weather has begun.

Wreck of the *Javanese Princess*

Which was not really wrecked, thanks to his care –
like Timex, MDR, the factories
he nearly kept on course, precision engineer
of inner mechanics, family's or crew's;
placer of the Captain's Apple, thus,
to tempt the Auld Man, bunneted, remote dictator,
to equilibrium and the Equator.

– Except in memory, mine, in which it's sunk
to childhood's sea-change of the names, routes, tales
that meant I hailed all Sinbad's as not bunk
but bunk-mates, and Ulysses' hungry betrayals
if not as pearls then surely fish-eye jewels.
Three circumnavigations, of which six ports
I approach in periplus via his reports.

Listing as we list, listening for the bell
that Graham heard in Greenock on the quay
and James in prison, asking, 'quhat thee befell':
Dundee's doppelbar I'd like to place
in Brooklyn by Moore's Camperdown elm tree; as
that drowning's set in the Demerara's night
where two drunk sailors fought and swamped their boat.

My world formed in his eavesdrop – *Stilla Maris* –
so I send him next through Suez and not Panama
from ship-star Polaris on to *Octan*'s Australis,
stepping on deck post-Eden's psychodrama,
his whites sweat-drenched in Red Sea seconds; from clamour
of such docks I have him enter the Officers' Club
on the Hooghly where, here's the nub, none such would rub

shoulders with their Empire's enablers: Dundee's
jutewallahs; these, in turn, would rarely leave
their St Andrew's Dinner compounds, yet learn Hindi
post-Independence, so, when he arrives

a curry can be cooked by someone's wife
who isn't European, though I missed
both the host's name and the small hopefulness of this.

– Perhaps because I loved drink taken's boasts,
those barnacles on the hull of every story
such as the rest upon the route of ghosts,
that midnight maze of docks at Kidderpore
for stotted wits till, woken by his own snores,
he found a railway sleeper was his bed,
dawn's first train nearing where he'd laid his head.

Each tale retold is doubled, so it is
his globe is spun into a variorum:
my voyages all shadowings of his;
each book's keel echoing his currents' programme,
this idiot prow the ninth to join that quorum
and write some more on water since he's lost,
heart's constancy and lungs both commerce-tost.

Thus, dry-docked in Whampua, why embark
on how a shipmate, docked a day for absence
said, 'Eh'm anely back tae cheenge my sark –
Jist dock me twa' – except that mock defiance
delays my end and is my whole defence
against his inhaling there, like Osaka blossom,
asbestos wool and, thus, the whole abysm.

sark: shirt.

ALGOS

We distinguish life from death, but in my opinion things are not how they are explained to us. I believe that they are different for each person, like dreams. I think that to reach an understanding of death first we must understand the distinct places that exist within us, and dreams are one of these places.

LEONORA CARRINGTON

The Tortoise

(Mansoor Hotel, Hargeysa)

The tortoise is as slow as any boulder
faced with the horizontal.
It bumps along the path
between the hotel bungalows

with its head like an elderly baby
flinching when the shell knocks
against the high concrete verge.
I peer into its pebble eye:

the next tear looks a decade away.
Am I startling it into flight? If so,
the precipitate has become imperceptible.
Is a day an hour to a tortoise, or is

an hour a day? A well-cudgelled skull
escaping from a giant's grave,
it discovers the end of the path,
and its front feet try to climb

out of our world altogether.
They scratch out a route
that the shell fails to follow,
clunking like the hull of a boat

whose owner wants to fish on land.
Kin to both crystal and cauliflower,
the colour of dirt so dry it could be sand,
the shell can't reach the rocking point

and slides back. The tortoise takes
another run at it, glancing at me
as time passes, like an irritable old man
being driven through a crowded market.

This time it finds the shell's fulcrum
and rocks there, hind legs seeking purchase
as your hand would grope behind a curtain
for the window's latch. Finally, one claw

attracts the concrete lip's attention
and sends the tortoise crashing
into the dust of the garden
like an engineless car arriving

in the skeleton of Eden. Another age
passes: governments topple
with far less grace. Then
its ancient head is born again.

Kalighat

A red dog lies in the red dye dust
of the stalls-lined lane to Kalighat.

Somewhere over my shoulder a goat
is going to heaven. Four young men
trampoline it into hot air from a blanket
till it gets the idea. I don't notice,
but someone tells me later. The red dog
lies in the dyed red dirt: what colour is
the red dog really? What colour is the dirt?
How dirty is dirt, really? The goat keeps
being thrown from the throat of the street
up in anticipation of its translation
which it isn't looking forward to.

I don't notice but afterwards presume
it points its hooves neatly toward the earth
each time, but now we both must enter
the continuity of Kalighat. My elbow
is touched by an elderly person
who points out to it that there are poor
people hereabouts. Through the eye
of the entrance, threaded with a thick braid
of worshippers, goats and traders, a Brahmin
catches my eye. The red tongue of Kali,
triangular, electric, points our way.

The buildings' blocks have been so neatly
slotted into the temple complex that
there must be a tourniquet of queueing
wound around hall and kitchen
and the slatted wall of the slaughter place
just to get anywhere the priest
wants to point out to us past the echo
less note that is the striking of a blow.
On an occasion like this many will die
and the meat be distributed among
the mostly vegetarian – here he seizes us

and one by one inserts us in the alley –
at eye level the sanctum is packed
with people and smoke. A girl swings back
and forth from a slim pillar above me,
her eyes on something over my shoulder,
and between the busy lattice of limbs
I see a little pyramidal stone amid flames,
an upended pudendum until I ask
was that Her? as I am plucked out
and a new witness is aligned. Until I ask,
after, by the ghat's oblong soup,

how many veins of her red thread
are being wound around my wrist?

Ganesh is Reading

In the glorious tat-stacked Kerala State tourist shop
Lord Ganesh is reading a sandalwood book.
He is supine, reclining on a couch or sunlounger,
and, though no doubt the tome is sacred,
he's casual, because that's his style, man:
grey man with a leg on his face, spiritual truth
is like holiday reading to him – allegory
and parable are genre. While we feel them
all over and answer with partials: Western Snake,
Detective Palm Tree, Sci-fi Sail, the Side
of a Romantic Tent, drumming in that urgent gale –
his pulse of beginnings and beings and being
no more – to him it is as clear as sweat,
since he remembers the first raindrop, how
shy they all pretended it was, and knows
the final tear, how the face it will fall from
will not be human at all, and what this will mean.
Ganesh is absorbed by the fragrance of the text
though the carver has left the page blank;
he snuffs it all over with his sandalwood nose
and knows the unwritten the way we suppose
a God can listen to all our epics and raags
before their authors were even composed,
when all there was was the anticipation of sand,
a prophecy of water and a blank page of the sun
slowly turning in colours that would have to wait
for their names. Ganesh likes the way we were right
on time with those, needing no prompt to call
the sunset papaya, the clouds abalone, the sun
a sliced chilli, then the peppercorn stop of night.

The Losers' Table

> I look around at us and you know what I see? Losers...
> I mean, like, folks who have lost stuff.
>> *Guardians of the Galaxy Vol. 1*

It had already been raining and was promising more
like the raised pad of an elephant's foot
when we came out from the lacquered teak chest interior
of Adishakti's mud-brick theatre like wrong notes;

it was already dark and the pineapple-large lamps
were lit above the two round tables where we sat outside
between translation and after rehearsal – one the good table
for chai and morning papers if you've done your yoga;

the other for losers, stacking bottles and glasses and lighters
Babel-high on late night malt, gin and nimboo
and the remains of rum, as though some buried lodestone drew
the worse half of us toward midnight's court

to hear our sentence from our own drowned mouths –
the between-rain air like a long gulp of breath
had pulled with it hundreds of forefinger-length, soft-winged bugs,
cotton come to life, ash aloft: they gathered in white night flakes

about the dizzy lightbulbs dangling across the yard, as though
peeled away from the kernels of those incandescent globes:
all swarm, unstill, not focusable upon until
each white-hot needle body, caught up in its solo swirl,

seemed nothing but flight, less definite than its own shadow
on our skin as we moved among them, not listening to us
but caught up in the rhetoric of light, colliding with, unsettling on
our arms, the up-reach of our palms, in our hair and on our faces,

gathering and shredding haloes and wings about us like all
our scribblings turned inside out, all punctuation shaken loose – no bail,
just a jailbreak of the dozen languages we'd ganged together,
imagoes of all the shibboleths we'd had to let go of

to sit down here, to drink together and to be at one.

Four Songs in the Guangling Style, and a Signature

I *'Wine Madness'*

We gather to hear the master in an office block.
That the lift is a sort of raw crate lined
with plywood and ripped posters offers
a contemporary contrast to the soundboard of *firmiana*
simplex, or parasol wood, the base of *catalpa ovata*
from which he has made his 古琴 (*gǔqín*).
At the end of a street-long corridor
we are greeted by a grinning man in black slippers
who offers us tea and Moutai in little cups.

II *'Wild Geese on a Sandy River Bank'*

The master sits in the calligrapher's studio
as though he has been waiting for six drunkards
and Xi Chuan for a thousand years,
his hands resting in the space he has folded
as neatly as rice paper between the music.
After several further cups of Moutai, there is
a debate about whether the syllable 麗 (lì)
adds elegance to the adjective 美麗 (měilì)
which takes longer than his song to resolve itself.

III *'Confucius after the Death of his Favourite Student'*

He continues to play the silence
with the side of his finger and not the nail
in the Guangling style. We continue to drink Moutai.
There is a character formed by three leaves of tea
in my teacup. Xi Chuan explains
that either it is 风 (fēng) and means 'wind',
or it is 爪 (zhǎo) and means 'claw',
or it is 介 (jiè) and means 'between'.
We are loudly shooshed by the company.

IV *'The Woodcutter's Song'*

The last piece is impossible to play
without a gathering of 氣 or *qì* energy.
The music's intention must live alongside
the chance accompaniment of our mobiles,
trilling like robot canaries, the squeak of our mouse shoes;
the tea's pouring and the toilet's post-tea pouring,
the traffic in the long midnight street,
and the traffic's eager horn section.
The grinning man has discovered another bottle.

V *'Three Day Monk'*

How the slippered man pouring *cha* and *baijyoh*
throughout the *gǔqín* master's performance
turned out to be the great calligrapher
        whose studio this was.

How he then ripped and folded ricepaper
casually into two strips of seven squares
each with a saltire of folds to hold
        the heart of each character.

How he with dip and splash and drag conflated
music, alcohol, and era into a poem thinking itself
back to life on paper, drawing the room's groan
        out with a single upward stroke.

How he repeated this, discarding its perfection
in search of rougher gestures, still more human
for catching on our grain, a falling back he signed
        and rolled and gave to me.

Nanjing Nightboat

To be on the nightboat not quite drunk
as it pulls away from the Confucian arch
stating 'Literature is the backbone of the universe';

from the red gold inner lit plastic boat stop sign,
from the examination hall and the blue neon wave effect,
the car showroom's cross-eyed dragon twins.

To pass beneath the bridge an elephant claims
to support, and by the isle of giant exploding goldfish,
the trio of trumpeting flower arches, and leave

the statue of Li Bai's liver to cradle the moon,
the clothing monsters hanging in half-lit windows,
and the motorcycles watching us from balconies.

Is to watch the water remember how to ripple,
its long tubular wake, its reticule of electricity –
light finely chopped as dofu, its mercury eels;

its seeds of moonflowers, cold toads' throat boilings,
petals on its surface as though they were just any leaf –
the water is being lit when it doesn't require it.

But it bears us on without resentment, jasmine
still allows itself to trail down into it,
willow swings its thinning strands as

we pass beyond into an endlessness of river,
black and lined with spangled black, moonless,
every ripple like clean bone and lithe as a bow.

The Two Haircuts

(for Nikola Madzirov)

isn't really about the haircuts, but
the walk home after the banquet
after the haircuts, and not really home
but a hotel, but not the hotel where
on the special executive 26th floor

the richest man in Tianjin, far too familiar
with very sharp knives, had carved
cured Iberican ham-flakes off
an almost entire leg, then bared
his tattooed chest and belted out karaoke.

He didn't have any Johnny Cash
so we left. At least the Moon was cool
on our newly shaven skulls, the streets
deserted except for the two women
outside the 24 hour foot massage

(12 hours per foot) who put us back
on the right track. The high buildings' grime
was hidden by the greater grime of night
as though light was clean; the windows
were all barred at this depth, grilles

on the aircon units. Then long stretches
with no cars, back streets' grid like grooves
in a square record, vinyl of the seventies,
sticking on a lull from the Tang dynasty,
not unlike that village where the deaf mute

had cut Nikola's hair with one pair of scissors
and half a comb, the same one where
the previous year in Pig Heaven Inn
I'd listened to a dark ocarina. But that had been
long before all the aforementioned befores.

Many haircuts had flowed below our collars'
itchy bridges since then. Which is when we knew
that we were lost, and sat at the crossroads
letting others hunt for taxis, and rubbed
our nearly hairless heads, rueful with delight.

An Exotic Dream of Leonora Carrington

Once in the tiny wee small hours I was moving through the forest with a troupe of eyeless clowns, and the branches whispered '*Alebrije, alebrije...*'.

The clowns had no idea where they were going, and continually smacked into tree trunks. Despite this, they refused to slacken their pace.

The forest was quiet, apart from the whimpering of the concussed clowns. Even though no one knew where we were going, we made steady progress.

In this forest, not even the trees knew which direction was north, and accordingly they grew moss in an opportunistic manner.

And now dried porridge oats began to fall gently, resting on the conifers and sticking to the blood-and-chalk faces of the eyeless clowns.

As one the smeary-faced clowns turned to face me. We were in a clearing being pelted with porridge. What did they want – guidance? Or to feast?

From the clowns' eyesockets crawled little robot scorpions, but instead of stings they had pulsing scarlet whoopee cushions, lit from within, that farted and reinflated.

I took that to mean everything was OK. I felt for my phone, but in my pocket was a broken crispbread. As I looked up, the Moon whipped past overhead, then whipped past again.

Teatro Orfeon

On Sueñoday, Dead Leonora insists that we go, please,
to the Orfeon on Calle Luis Moya to see the z-movies,
those films never actually made that are only the dreams
of failures and recluses – 'Like you!' she exclaims.

It's like someone hammered an Art Deco facade
onto a difference engine, but in any old iron,
then an Antikythera mechanism was placed
here, and the Tōnalpōhualli put there. '*Nota bene,*'

she says ' You don't mind if I call you Benny?
We must sit with our backs to the screen
while it extracts ten thousand fears, adds tamarisk,
and fakes our lost hopes. Then, insert a Phaistos disc.'

*

The skeleton tries to sleep in the consoling
darkness of fat, floating within its lake of skin
till muscles' harnesses grip it again
and morning comes in through the usual holes.

The mosquito gondoliers stand ankle-deep
in pulque, stingers for poles, in the metro they keep
beneath the metro, where their gondolas trundle
on hundreds of hard rubber wheels.

*

The Orfeon's title card reads I USED TO HAVE A BRAIN
THE SIZE OF A POET. JE RÉPÈTE... She yells into its gears,
'Roll the next film!' I see her silhouette between
those of jackal-headed mantises and sexton bears.

*

The giantess pushes her bicycle through
the grid of the Histórico Centro –
some streets are too narrow for her tyres,
so as though her handlebars were

metal moustaches she leans over and bellows
'Amateurs!' at the pedestrians below.
She reaches a skyscraper, opens a door
the exact height of the skyscraper, and goes to work.

*

'Dead Remedios said the city was anti-centripetal
beginning with a newborn's navel and proceeding
into a human palm. In between it's all centipede.'
'Could you remove your hand from my thrapple?'

'If you insist, but it's come a long way for this.'
'Pray continue.' 'A public service announcement first.'
THE RABBIT GODS ADVISE TO PULL BACK
A LITTLE ON THE PULQUE. 'Is this not milkshake?'

*

Lowry returns home in his cactus crown
down the Avenidas Amsterdam. Either uneasy lies
the head that wears the cactus, or uneasily
it tells the truth. Or is it that from chin to frown

all is cactus? Whichever, he is not permitted
to take it off. He staggers a little, his cream three-piece
streaked with cream. At the foot of the holy tree
is a heap of plastic bags full of dogshit.

*

'Never mind the Herzogs, or Kubrick's wallpaper-
licking Bonaparte, what you need is Harpo,
leading the charge from *Giraffes on Horseback Salad*
of the Roast Chicken Brigade, upon a porcelain saddle.'

LAUREL'S SCRIPTS FEATURING DEAD OLLIE:
THE GHOST CHILDREN LOVE THOSE. 'Or Keaton's *Grand Hotel*
extending forever through its always-different foyers,
bars crammed with darkness, follies, sharpers, and valises,

gobstoppered with bored lights, where nine hundred blank
but terribly handsome extras in nightshirts blink
in a monochrome kaleidoscope of drive-through wardrobes,
indoor Sonoras, and fathomless rooftop Las Pozas...'

She sinks back into her gelid seat as these precise images
play across the skinless perfection of her grimace.
I realise that silently and without being seen
the entire theatre has rotated to face the screen.

Keaton in Space

Since it is black and white and absolutely silent
since his death Keaton has been travelling between
the stars. At first he could pull railroad track out
of his carpet bag as far as Jupiter, where he fell
from the footplate of The Great Leveller into
the blind spot of the eye of the Great Red Spot.

As he fell he replaced each pork pie hat torn from
his head with a pork pie hat he rapidly fashioned
from a stetson using a thick paste of sugar water,
clapping it onto his head as soon as it dried only
for it to be removed at once by his terminal velocity
all the long while of miles of staring straight down.

Around him on all sides were stacks of jalopies
and paddle steamers whirling and crashing together,
hand-cranked cameras still shooting, thickets of mikes,
lighting rigs like blazing sails on gyring schooners,
the fife-rail of one of which he hooked himself to
by a shoe-tip, and steered for Saturn's celluloid rings.

After a lonesome century pursuing himself by handcar
around their gritty circuit, getting so close sometimes
as to grab his own shoulder, only to shrug off
the distraction, he tired of the back of his own head
and boarded a giant eyeball, immersing himself
in salt jelly and embarking on night's longest stare.

After thousands of years of still being dead,
the SS *Beckett* brought him forth from the Zone of Teleos,
and he forgot there ought to be a reason for
his voyaging, forgot he was anything but a beetle
rolling an eyeball from darkness to darkness,
and dreamed that he was filming this again.

Lion in Sidecar

(for Pedro and Richard)

It's a black and white wall of death,
breathless with blur: you can almost hear
the fleet trundle of the motorcycle wheels
on the cheap plywood planks –
it's a barrel of roar.

The lion is really getting into it
at ninety degrees to vertical:
leaning into the rush of air,
eyes slitted, mane flaring like
the Sun in a speeded-up, unhinging orrery,
like Jean Marais in the underworld's gale.

Begoggled Heurtebise bears him bravely, always
upward, though the lion knows
in these realms up is always
down. Does the lion know
where he is going? Does the lion know

where we are going? Our animal stares straight ahead
as the cycle ascends to the watchers along the brim.

Mother Goo

McGueegueg smoothed the lacquered sneer of his quiff
and slid a harpoon-like forearm along the seatback,
rippling the russet leather billows of his Ford Peyote.
Ron Maelstrom shrugged it off, not having been driven in
to a showing of *20,000 Leagues* for this. Half-turning
in protest, he took in the green jelly tsunami which quivered
behind them, police cars pulsing in its bio-luminescent maw,
and permitted himself a single elongated squeak.
Steve sneaked out the parking lot while Mother dined.
Since Chief Ernest Borg had been assimilated, who
would lead the town? Running down its tinsellated drag,
waving in a frenzy at the friendly uninitiated shoppers,
he crashed into Captain Rehab, the bear-hearted rogue
who had, during long spells in the state asylum, inscribed
scenes from his inner voyages upon his own incisors,
which he bared now, thirstlessly and stinking of myrrh:
'Stevie boy, what's your hurry? Don't you like me?'
McQueegueg indicated the now aurora-large bulbous invader,
nine splay-limbed consumers hanging in her midst
as in a macedoine, emitting a perfume of macerated cake.
Immediately Rehab drew his Magnum and took aim:
there were a series of luckless punks as the shells hit home –
though one took out a partially digested Anabaptist.
'She don't mind the perforations,' Steve explained as
they reversed a 4 x 4 before her avenue-devouring mass.
Meanwhile, excreted onto a parkbench and inexplicably
wearing his neighbour's kimono, blinged with gunk,
Maelstrom vomited Goo's innards in the bin, noting
they went down in a spiral like a foie gras galaxy.
His mind was brilliantly cleared, as though nano-Buddha
had gone through it with a nailbrush, leaving nothing.
Around him, like freshly laundered zombies, townsfolk
with more or less all their limbs and faces, lurched
toward their houses, emptied of Christmas but left
with its spirit, far too neat. He watched the space-saliva
race like green mercury about his limbs before finding
an orifice and slipping in. He was totally wormed.

In the drained fountain was a banjo, fashioned from
the shell of a sea turtle, still warm from the tuning:
he strummed it and sang the shanties of that species
which will follow us down Mother's universal gullet.

The Fathership

The Faithership is sinkin fast
tho anely intae uts ain past
while engineers regardyloo
uts captain crehs abandon crew!
Ye never met a morphosis
as rigidly applehd as this:
destroyer, whaler, clipper, barque,
galleon, galley, Argo, Ark.
The Faithership, the Faithership!
Full fathom fifty – on it slips!

Still at the helm tho ut pints richt doon,
hummin 'Resurgam', an auld-farrant tune,
oor Cap kens merchants that nae langer breathe –
Atlantean affshore accoonts a-seethe
tae trade in whale sushi, last seepins o ile
fur mirlins o plestic and nuclear spile.
The Faithership, the Faithership!
The Mariana Trench fur yir rubbish tip.
First fill up thi seas syne tak tae the skehs,
set sail fur Mars, thon billionaires' prehz!

For as ut sinks uts rats wull rehz
swellin oan fructage o fascist lehz,
clingin tae spars o colonial cane
and speirin whit wey can't we dae ut again?
Behold thir fleet sans hope or sopite,
a flotsam o sin that's soppin wi spite;
a rottach aroond ilka mooth i the rammy,
gorgin on guts they unfold fae gold lamé.
The Faithership, the Faithership!
Aim at the lifeboats! Let grapeshot rip!

Holes haloed wi grease and hoolin wi greed –
the seas ur a-heavin whaur hellejays feed
whaur sharks hae a hoolie but wha wad ye save
amang sooravoolics when here's the Ninth Wave?

79

Here comes thi wan tae sweep aathin awa,
mak Jesus and Mary and jetsam of aa.
The Faithership, the Faithership!
He hung up His Son syne geed um thi slip:
Eloi Eloi lama sabachthani?
Kick oot the jammy pieces, Mammy!

The Faithership – ye hud tae query –
wiz aye designed as tapsalteerie:
uts parent company, Poseidon,
is a shell fur the shills o thi Upside Doon.
Oor surplus cargo drifts ashore
tae ensure the poor hae Scotch galore,
while oor herniatin honk o voices
sall drouk yir *nisi* fou o noises.
The Faithership, the Faithership!
Hoo sall we wauken fae this bad trip?

The Faithership, the Faithership:
wha sall loosen its auld man's grip?
tae thrapples, lapels, tae reins, tae guns,
he'll niver let gae till the West is un-won.
Saturn merely swallied'iz weans –
Droont Dad'll growe gills tae haud oantae his gains.
The Faithership, the Faithership!
Wha sall loosen its deid man's grip?
Auld Man o the Sea, Youth's scorpion ride
He'll no let gae till the Yirth huz died.

Regardyloo: after Gardyloo ('Look out for the water'), a warning in Edinburgh when waste was thrown from a window into the street; *pints*: points; *auld-farrant*: old-fashioned; *mirlins*: small particles; *speirin*: asking; *sopite*: settlement (Scots law); *rottach*: a circular dirty mark around the mouth or the hem of a garment; *hellejay*: the razorbill; *hoolie*: a wild party; *sooravoolic*: cadger, chancer; *jammy pieces*: bread and jam; *tapsalteerie*: head over heels; *nisi* (νίσι): island [Greek]; *thrapples*: throats; *weans*: children; *Yirth*: Earth.

JESUS MARY AND JETSAM 1

But their eyes were holden that they should not know him.

LUKE, 24: 16

Verbotentotentanz

T'ain't no sin
To take off your skin
And dance around in your bones...
WILLIAM BURROUGHS,
The Black Rider

1

At first, owing to the absence
of a tongue or larynx, no one knew
what the skeleton was saying

but gradually the dry pattern
of clacks resolved into the skeleton
of words in urgent tarantella.

The fire pretended those brow ridges
were expressive, so we imagined
the sun at noon, casting light

in two shafts through those sockets.
Each bone, it was saying, has
another skeleton within it

formed after after. Look, here's mine,
it clicked, and, plucking a rib, curiously
pierced, it put it to its no-lips

and, somehow, began to play.

A Jesus of the Moon

(variation on a theme by Nick Cave)

Jesus lived with Diana and a rabbit
on the moon. It was like all the deserts
rolled up into a ball so he was fine with that:
'If I can do forty days and forty nights
then I can do four billion years,' he would say
to the Goddess stroke Princess.

Theirs was a chaste relationship: sometimes he
would chase the rabbit, skin and roast it;
sometimes it would chase him, screaming,
'This is your flesh! This is your blood!'
Then Diana would hunt them down with a bow
and a moon-buggy, which neither thought fair.

On the Dark Side they would curl up together
and suckle from her sixty-four nipples;
His beard would retreat into his long soft ears,
and the rabbit would dream in parables.
Theirs was a relationship as complete
as the panels in a long-running cartoon:

each panel felt like a carriage on the Trans-
Lunar Express, in which they would cantillate
to the seaside that best suited their mood:
Silence, Tranquillity, Concupiscence.
Once they found a hairless rockstar, crying
in a crater, and Jesus repaired his bicycle.

Each month the rockstar would wait
by the track, and, as their train went by
(the carriages painted with the company logo:
a carrot on a crucifix over crossed arrows,
all inside a demi-lune), he would pedal as
fast as he could alongside, and wave.

Emmaus, 1997

On the stairwell in the Mater Hospital
hangs a Velázquez print from the series
called *bodegones*, or 'inns', looking much like
a dark cupboard I barely glanced into then
because I had to go to the pub on the corner

and wait with Liam for the Guinness to settle
and the right words to come about my father:
do you think he'll live? And in the print
a woman won't glance up from the pewter,
her handcloth like a fried egg on the table,

nor looked out for us as we climbed the stairs
to news or just the hope of news, his face drained
of blood for weeks on end as, my age now,
he lay there, loosely filling in 'liver' on the menu.
They brought out hot sausages as we drank

his health, and we ate them with mustard.
But in the top left corner of the *bodegone*,
as though another picture in an earlier style
were hanging behind her, is a serving hatch
that opens on the supper at Emmaus.

Jesus, master of the once removed, Who might
have sat among us as we drank or indeed was
that woman serving from her far country,
Who might be before me now or any surgeon here,
could You make Yourself known at the bar?

A Jesus of the Mammoths

When Jesus lived among the mammoths
he thought as a mammoth
and had hair like a mammoth.
Also a monobrow.

Spiders wove his garments from mammoth wool as
it floated over the meadows and caught
in the wild grasses, for none of the grasses
had been tamed yet.

He kept far from the haunts of people
for they did not yet have souls
and so there was nothing he could do for them.
Therefore he stayed among the gentle mammoths
who were on their way out.

Basically, once you develop a soul
that's you, so they send for Jesus.
No, I don't know who 'they' are either,
are you not going to lift a finger here?

– How unlike the homework of our own dear mammoths
who gladly hoisted a trunk to construct,
according to Jesus's design, scratched on larch bark,
a mansion on the permafrost with many rooms
built of timber, tusks, tears, and bones.

Did I mention that Jesus's nose was grey
and scored with horizontal lines
but that he otherwise resembled Cesare Borgia,
and that he sometimes wore a dress
patterned with the wild flowers of the plains:
blue squill, Arctic dock, alpine bearberry,
and the herbaceous plant *Silene stenophylla*?
No, I see that I did not.

Many thousands of mammoths perished
constructing this palace in which it was taboo
for anything corporeal to set foot:
'Their spirits shall dwell in my Father's house forevermore,'
Jesus would murmur, though at that point
'forevermore' indicated ten thousand years –
a mere blurt in geological time.

God could have put him straight on this in an instant,
but prayer had not yet been invented, and so
Their lines of communication were poor.

'In a way,' Jesus would later reflect, 'it was the best of times,
because I had to make it up as I went along.'
'You're forgetting the dinosaurs,' God interrupted,
'before I sent in The Meteor.'
'Oh God, the dinosaurs!' Jesus laughed,
turning a little green. '*Could* they build an ark?'
They were both laughing helplessly now.
'Never do a trial run on Original Sin!'

Meanwhile, on the mammoth steppe,
bereft of counsel, of His gentle face,
the final mammoths nudged at the mossy walls,
their massive foreheads crammed
as though a stomach full of grasses
with memory after memory after memory.

The Muriels

Muriel made a note to call Muriel to look after the cats
while she was visiting Muriel in Monifieth. Muriel could tell
the other Muriels she wouldn't make their monthly meeting.

The Six Muriels they had called them at school, or rather
Miss McClennan had, for she had been a Muriel too, as well
as their history teacher, and was alluding to the original six,

maidservants to the much-pestered Muriel, Queen of Scots.
They had always been on hand, as it were, to thrust an arm
through the door-staples in castle after castle, or so it seemed,

thinking back to the inefficient viciousnesses of the past.
She made a note to get the oven cleaned on her return.
How she had come to know the further, farther-away Muriels

she couldn't always recall – it wasn't as though she had sought
them out, or that there was a network of Muriels, passing on
their details, or gathering in certain known tearooms –

except, in a sense, thanks to coincidence, or fate, call it
what you will, now there was. She put the pencil down, but
its scratching continued. Thinking how her handwriting

aged her, she ran through her list of all the Muriels.
It comforted her, like a prayer, as indeed did the company
of Muriels. It wasn't as though they were all alike, oh no,

some Muriels were scatty as fruit bats, and others
scarcely worthy of the name Muriel. But, on the whole,
you could rely on a Muriel, or at least she had had to,

after the Terrible Year, or The Affair With or Of Muriel
McAlmond's man, Archibald McAlmond. Airchie.
She had called it by other names at the time:

The Aberration in Aberfeldy, or The Aftermath
To Mither, or The Fifty Seven Year Airch. (Although
Mum had been a Muriel too, she could never think of her

as such). She was able now to see it for what it was:
not a passion but the furor of its passing, perhaps forever –
God knows she wouldn't want that again. Or knew.

She glanced at the little icon of Muriel, Mother of God,
on the windowsill, but Her back was turned and She
was blessing the bird table. How she'd shuddered at

Her shrill voice accusing her from every church till
she couldn't go in, till the birds themselves began chanting
'Muriel' at dawn, slandering her from the onset of the light.

The woodpigeons were the worst: they had learned
her surname, and repeated it until it lost all meaning,
as if semantic satiation was all she was allowed:

McAllister McAllister McAllister. Later she had learnt
which of them had been at it too – the Muriels, not the birds.
For whom it was a matter now, though no comfort there for

poor Muriel McAlmond. She closed her eyes. Though this too
was not praying, it was more like it. Time to pack. McAllister
McAllister McAllister. The bus wouldn't wait for her.

A Jesus of the Beetles

> The Creator, if He exists, has an inordinate fondness for stars and beetles.
>
> J.B.S. HALDANE

One morning all the Beatles awoke
from their syncopated dreams
to find Jesus staring at them
from a chair at the foot of their bed.

'Why's he making those big eyes
at you, Paul?' John asked. 'If
he made Big Ears he'd be Noddy,'
Ringo replied. 'Did we even go to sleep

here?' asked George, who was really
not recognising the wallpaper.
'You weren't sleeping,' said Jesus,
'you were dead.' 'Not again!'

said Paul. 'Not you,' said Jesus.
'Not yet,' said Ringo. The wallpaper,
wisely, said nothing. It displayed
a wide variety of beetles dressed

as nineteenth-century hussars
performing their songs. Blue Rose
Chafers held each other's forelimbs;
Fortune Stag Beetles took labryses

to flat pack furniture; and Giant Unicorn
Beetles drove Bentleys into potholes.
Five-Horned Rhinoceros Beetles were
swallowing swazzles on molehills,

while Great Diving Beetles descended under-
water skelters, tiny medlars in their feelers;
Click and Violet Dor Beetles warred,
Rickenbacker contra argent hammer;

and crossdressing Dung Beetles
got back to rolling up the sun.
In the corner was our old reel-to-reel
on a woven rush-topped stool

and on that was the album Mum
used to play she can't recall now
but Jesus knows. 'Which album
was it, Jesus?' Paul asked

but Jesus just indicated how
the bulky green tape recorder
with its plastic picnic hamper handle
really was a Darkling Beetle: up

it buzzled like an asteroid or bullet.
'You know you're bigger in the flesh than
in the Bible?' John yawned. 'Depends'
said Jesus, 'on the size of the Word.'

The Lost Poem

(for Julia Darling)

Your real elegy is somewhere among my papers
in the way something of your death is in

that photo where the wrought iron dragon's shadow
falls across your face in an archway in

Barcelona; in the way you almost allow it.
Some, you see, were stored in the cellar

in the Low Lights, with its barrels and its ghost,
and nobody knows where they've gone. The lost

poem was about the ferry going out at night between
the two lighthouses, its stern like a pyramid

of lights shrinking as it crossed the bar, taking us
with it as though death were a continent,

as though we could visit you there, as though
the poem could be found, as though it were you.

Verbotentotentanz

2

Meh skeleton twin
buried within
yir brither o skin
we ken in yir banes
thi wey you alane
will ootlive me
sae furgive me
fur maakin ye bathe
in bluidy claiths.

Hoo close ye follae
this craitur sae hollae
as tho ye'd been swallied
beh yir ain whale
hoo sune Eh wull fail
and then ye can leh
lyk a lidless eh
defiant o dearth
fleeshed wi aa Yirth.

THE WRECK OF THE FATHERSHIP

All night the short waves talk
to the silent dark
but the dark comprehends it not
nor the silence
round the last corner of time
for beyond the bar over the Gaa Sands
the Mona has rolled over her crew

WILLIAM MONTGOMERIE

The Wreck of the Fathership

I

My father was never old
not even on his deathbed
his hair still boyish across
the brow I kissed him on,
brown as broken reeds
rising in Tay's afternoon light,
swaying in the pelvic curve
of the harbour at Broughty Ferry.

The Boat

Life-boat MONA a 45′6″ x 12′6″
Watson cabin Life-boat
with twin engines, each of 40 h.p.
built by Messrs Groves & Guttridge
at Cowes in 1935.

Nineteen boats of that class built
between 1927 and 1935.
This their first disaster.
Crews always spoke highly
of their sea-keeping qualities.

Her sister ship at Longhope
crossed the Pentland Firth
both ways against the tidal stream
on the 7th December in a whole gale
(force 10 to 11).

A complete survey of hull and engines
carried out at Weatherhead's boatyard
at Cockenzie between 9th December 1957
and 19th March 1958.
The hull opened up and water-tested.

The general condition was good
with no structural defects or decay.
Both engines removed
and completely stripped down
coolers and propeller shafts also removed.

Everything found to be in good order.

The engines last air-tested for water tightness
on the 24th and 25th of November.
No machinery failures reported in the boat
over eight years.

The life boat was taken out on exercise
and tested by the Northern District Inspector
on the 27th October
and by the Northern District Engineer
on the 5th December 1959.

III

The yellow man was doomed and knew it,
announced it to all comers in the eggbox ward.
He had a nozzle or a clip upon his swollen
abdomen, as though he was packaging, and
wasn't quite yellow, more a sore orange,
bald and dry-mouthed grapefruit, tender,
needing the curtains drawn, the curtains opened,
going home to die within the week and wanting
our company while he had it – how guilty
Dad and I were to talk about recovery.

The Assembling of the Crew

In the early hours of Tuesday December 8th
a strong south-easterly gale blowing across
the entrance to the Tay, flood tide to the westward.
Off Fife Ness at 02.02, the North Carr Lightship
broke away from its main anchor
and started to drift in the gale and heavy sea.

The lightship was without engines, so
could not manoeuvre or move without tugs.
Situated at the turning point for entry into
both the Tay and Forth Estuaries,
the first lightship was positioned in 1887
and the '59 ship placed there in 1933.

The Fife Ness Coastguard first to spot
the lightship moving off station.
On board the North Carr, the Master,
Mr George Rosie, and crew
finally got another anchor over
at 06.45 approx. and stopped the drift.

Due to a combination of very low water
and the severe south-easterly, neither
Anstruther nor Arbroath Lifeboats could launch.
The coastguard telephoned for
the only lifeboat available
that could launch in any tide, the Mona.

At 02.42, Captain Norman Moug
received the message 'North Carr Lightvessel
drifting in north-westerly direction. Advise launch.'
He telephoned the Coxswain, Ronald Grant,
who lived at Cotton Road in Dundee, and also
the Lifeboat Mechanic, John Grieve, in Fisher Street.

John senior woke his son, also John,
then went across to the shed to fire the maroons.
John junior ran round to David Anderson's house

in King Street to wake him. Ronald Grant kissed
his wife and 18 month old daughter goodbye,
and phoned for a police car to pick him up.

V

He held up his hand and we watched it tremble
because of the too much oxygen in his brain
both curious and at that moment unafraid.
Then he asked for the curtain to be drawn because
the Fruzomide that eliminated water from
his tissues made him piss like a carthorse
and I couldn't help but catch a glimpse
as I handed him the bedpan made of the same
cardboard they use for cartons of eggs.
No more than odd I thought it then, how all these
seem linked – penis to womb to birth to tomb –
No odder than the fact I can't remember the tie
I chose for him, the one he'll never take off.

The Last Voyage

With the help of Head Launcher Charles Knight,
the Mona went down the slipway at about 03.13
Captain Moug reported that the launch went well.
The Mona sent her first R/T message to
the Fife Ness Coastguard at 03.20,
and made her way downriver at 6 knots.

They tried to call the North Carr without success.

The Lightship was sending up rockets at regular intervals
to give her position. At around 04.00
the senior coastguard at Carnoustie, David Mearns,
caught his first sight of the Mona as she cleared Buddon Ness,
she appeared to have reduced speed and was
constantly disappearing in the mountainous seas.

He watched as she crossed the bar of the Tay.

The North Carr Lightship fired another rocket
at 04.25 and the Fife Ness coastguard asked
if the Mona had seen it. 'No…our position…
We have just passed the middle buoys on the bar
and we are just hanging on.' Mearns saw the Mona
turn south into St Andrews Bay at about 04.45.

At 04.48 the Fife Ness coastguard radioed
that the North Carr had sent up a red rocket
and asked if the Mona had seen it. 'Yes we saw that one.
We have just cleared the bar.' That was the last message.

The coastguard saw her masthead light
in St Andrew's Bay at 05.39, so asked the lightship
if they could see the lifeboat? 'Yes,
I think it is the lifeboat, will burn another flare.'

The Fife Ness coastguard sent a signal
to the Mona on the distress frequency asking
if their receiver was working to fire rockets
and flash their searchlight up into the sky –

There was no response, and a few minutes later
the masthead lights disappeared.

Hopkinsian 1

Thrum of nerves' gansy,
jacketed in life, like a corslet,
zoster of flesh's inheritance of pangs,
bright with it against the buffet
of six foot news, the phone a lightship in your liquid
hand, breaking bell from anchor, core from comfort's
creel of continuity, swept up by raketide
not our time, wipewaves not our weave, choiceless, Kairotic, unchancy.

Eight bodies the firth ate
eight names Tay returned
with the doomed timbers of their stormed boat,
Mona, taken and burned
in the Forth for a witch who'd conjured up that fiend
that snaps all bonds – though we termed her Medea Upturned
that held her offerings under, till weaned
off air, all signal lost, they fed depths' appetite.

Eightsome's weight
reels in the water's tears
conglomerated by waves' sleights,
feet kicking at sea's gears
shifting from drift to draught, long swallowing down
of these two yards of life's fraught volunteers
those eight frail memories, now drowned
complete as flesh that flails, fails, and is made disparate.

Drowned in day's going
on and down and through
the bloody-mindlessness of doing
our heads damage, hearts' rue
made uniform, made daily, dutiful, gaunt
with your presence redrawn in new hi-vis routines,
your numen in luminescence's haunts,
the pier where your yearly wreaths appear, till flung on the flowing.

VIII

Eating sibling-quick, too socially,
the carry-out with guests, he rose
choking and I followed and just caught him
as he blacked out in deposition from host
to his diminished flesh, still striking
his pow on the toilet as we fell. At
that moment he leaves his body and
begins to watch not over us but
helplessly. Returned, his whispered shame.
That night, in the nine-months-before
same bed where the hospital will call me,
I understand how everything must fail.

The Discovery

At first light about 08.30 a search was organised
in which a shore party and a helicopter took part.

A barman from the Carnoustie Station Hotel
was the first person to reach the scene.

At first he thought it was a ship's small boat
come in with the storm. When he reached it

he shouted if there was anyone there, but
with no response. When he started to walk back

he saw a young man's body floating in the surf.
He tried to pull him in, but the corpse was too heavy.

Coastguard John Hamilton came along and together
they pulled the body up onto the sands.

That turned out to be the youngest member of the crew,
John T. Grieve. Hamilton was a Corporation employee

who was also a relief coastguard. When the rocket went off
he left his job and hurried to the coastguard station,

the others having already left for the Gaa Sands
with life-saving equipment. By walking

and cycling in turn along the wet sand, he arrived
before the others. Hamilton took part in both

the beginning and the end of the Mona's trip.
He had been on coastguard duty from 2am to 8

and he had received the message at 02.45
that the North Carr Lightship had broken adrift.

He called Senior Coastguard David Mearns
and the message was relayed to Broughty Ferry

to call out the lifeboat. Shortly after he had heard
the maroon being fired from Westhaven.

A message on the pad at the station told him
the Mona had been driven ashore at Buddon.

The Carnoustie Coastguard Station officer
was the first person to board the lifeboat.

This was about 09.20. He found five bodies
all wearing life-jackets. Of these, mechanic

John Grieve was half in and half out
of the engine room, the hatch being secured

in the open position. Three other bodies
were in the after shelter, two with their hands to port.

The fifth body was lying under the steering shaft,
abaft the steering position, head to port.

Half a mile to the southward of the lifeboat
was found the body of ex-coxswain Alexander Gall.

Near it was the lifejacket of George Watson
along with the broken foremast of the lifeboat.

All seven men died from drowning,
they suffered no injuries apart from abrasions.

The seven bodies were taken to
the police mortuary at Carnoustie.

The eighth, of George Watson, was never found.

Hopkinsian 2

Maimed for the job,
Father, and farther from you,
I never manned so much as a coble
nor broached on brine's undrinkable brew:
while you girdled the globe three times by twenty one
I finished a first degree; words, fathomless, drew
my thirstiness, thirstlessly gulping me down,
while horizons' languages, high bird-winged, hybrid, were yours to absorb.

Dad, did you ever
see it, the *rayon vert* –
ocean's green lantern sliver
on the sun, supposed to confer
virtue on its sunset watcher on foam?
So, standing at the bow off Java, you staged your stare
witnessing if not westering home-
ward, turning to savour the far East as your senses' saviour.

Whole sway of whales' see,
all verge-merge and nowhere road:
each snail trail wake a tear that self-enseals;
each week away a goad
to the bull-back *nostos*, that turns exile's axle,
at pains to pick ivory for the memory ship's hold
its portholes open to dream and the actual –
each memento's momentum carried home to and on through me.

Mind Dundee's twin –
how in New York and parched
from your first crossing you went in
thon Doppelgängin bar:
gantry, coonter, saadust, clientele,
whiskies, eighty shillin, pehs and aa
mirrors mirrorin – even *The Tully*,
since Dundee was everywhere, tho mebbe no thon evenin's.

The Tully: *The Evening Telegraph*, a Dundee newspaper

XI

He approached it methodically as though
he had a plan, the way through this
he'd mentioned to my uncle when he'd bought
the last newspaper he would read. Chicken,
salad, potatoes, all pushed in steadily, chewed,
the pudding spooned at a brisk pace, sipping
juice through a stubby straw, not looking
and maybe not tasting, the meal a blur, a mass
his innards would not have time to transmute.

The Telling of the Wives

Kathy Stuart, 20 year old fiancée of John junior, heard the rumour on the lunchtime train from Dundee to Broughty Ferry.

Mrs David Anderson was walking along Fisher Street when she heard people speaking about the lifeboat. She hurried into the station, and broke down when told that everyone was lost. A friend assisted her home.

George Watson's wife, Winnie, was at work as a nurse at the Armitstead Convalescent Home. When she heard, she had to be given a sedative. Later, her parents drove from St Cyrus to be with her.

Before officials could visit her, Mrs Grant, wife of the coxswain, heard the news on a radio bulletin.

Hopkinsian 3

Bone phone calls in night
not caring whom it wakes
summons in the hearthouse without light,
from loaned loam to the life's boat, to the wee broken
free lightship, from the dream of the hospital to inhospitable
bulbflash fact, from who loves you to *nosokomeio*'s rack,
from innocent dark that plastic horned devil
twitching you swift to the life switch: a pulse in the neck still but slight.

Old time death time
pouring from the telephone
that old let me give you religion line
filling your hopeless home
with that other time that washes all past time above
along with what declines of flesh and bone
what for the love of God's called love,
its crest a foam that crazes, engraving your stone in the mind.

Death you no go
area in your own word
till a telephone network of woe
tells us it's aye been wired
into our flesh, an armature whaur Dreid
and Grief can perch, those corbies from Death's byre de-gyring
to where you lie, non-gleid
amang grieshoch, absence in heart's foundry: Death you weirdo,

strange to us as a son
or daughter must sometimes seem
to their own parent, this self's cessation
an incarceration in dreams
which father and mother our dead back for us, othered
as our creation but somehow still them
or close – it's we who appear dumbfouthered
by not being quite us, estranged in sleep's imagination.

nosokomeio (νοσοκομείο): hospital [Greek].

XIV

My father's hand was larger of palm than mine
and shorter fingered, and the hairs on its back
were blond amid the grizzling of veins as though
it had previously been the claw of a bear but
instead it had handled the watchmaker's fine devices
and worked in the ship's bowels with hot gauges
as though he must calibrate the earth's turning from
its core, or adjust it in an orrery till all ran well,
so when he was dead and I'd never hold it again
I wanted to photograph my father's hand,
that capable creature, as it lay dead upon
the sheet – its heft, its knocks, its tendons, that still
held his intelligence, its tenderness and force.
But it had already taken on the gravity
of the depths, as though glimpsed in the wreck
of a sunken vessel, and would not submit
to record; as though to return with this report
would set the blood to bubbling in my veins.

The Report

It is clear from internal evidence
that the Lifeboat capsized.

This almost certainly caused
by the Lifeboat being thrown off course
and across the sea
some time between 05.15 and 06.00.
It was probably in the shallow water
just to the south of the entrance
to the Tay at the time.

The Lifeboat then appears to have drifted
bottom up in a north westerly direction
until her signal mast touched bottom
in the shallow water between Buddon Ness
and Carnoustie. This had the effect
of righting the boat.

The Mona sent her last R/T message at 04.48.
Calculations from the fuel levels
before and after the disaster
and the boat's consumption by the engines give
an earliest possible time of the capsize
at 05.15 and the latest time of 06.45.

The Lifeboat probably first got into difficulties
when approaching the bar.
After 04.06 the lifeboat reported
she was abeam of the Abertay Lightship –
the crew could not have been wholly certain
because of the absence of the navigational buoys
which had been blown off course.

Weather conditions were exceptionally severe.

The RNLI considers that the decision to launch
was in the circumstances a wholly correct one.

Hopkinsian 4

Rose, compass rose,
you wither on our memorials;
his wristwatch like his wrist has frozen,
its hands stilled as sandstone sails
under lichen's freight, cradle no trade winds,
the lykewake untolled by kirk or ship's bells.
Rose, death like a lodestone has pinned
you here, unspun, direction reduced to the north of moss.

Twelve-winded sky,
where is that one point at which
your dozen blows? Or is there an eye
of no-storm, from which they'd reach
in each direction? That one, far from all regard;
the first all safety's opposite, its fetch.
But the doldrum's twin to the all-windward:
twelve-facing out or in's still where we're sent to die.

The watched face tricks
as does the windrose,
translating durance into disc
as flower flattens globe,
implying time's direction could be altered.
Dad, you understood each minute's minute pose
and carried the present's port of latter-
day futures like a featureless portrait on your wrist.

What in us fails
to tell the time is past,
not stored in memory's mock clock coils
as punctual as ghosts?
The dead do not inhabit our machines:
no tooth or cog hangs clogged with their ticking host
arriving at already-has-beens;
no second's secondary, each midnight ticks itself to null.

XVII

I remember the nurse saying 'Goodbye'
to my father's dead body as I left, having
attempted a kiss which felt too formal,
as though I were being introduced to
this foreign ambassador, his corpse.
I considered this new armature of his
absence on which our family now hangs,
as though it will appear at every table
when we gather to eat. She said 'Goodbye'
tenderly, as we kiss a friend, although she
had only known the manner of his leaving.

The Burning of the Mona

Mona, the Broughty Ferry disaster lifeboat
in which eight men died, was burned secretly
on a dark beach at 4.30 a.m.

Only a handful saw the lifeboat –
'perfectly sound and seaworthy' – destroyed
on confidential orders phoned direct from London.

Flames crackled as families slept
in a tenement only 50 yards away –
unaware of the funeral pyre.

They only learned about it when they saw
the twisted charred metal of the ruin,
still smoking on the rocks at daybreak.

After dark on Thursday night the Mona
had been taken across the harbour basin
and moored just inside the protection wall.

Then about 4 am she was moved round
the sea wall, secured by two chains,
and left to settle on the rock-strewn foreshore

as the tide ebbed. She was set alight
and by daybreak all that was left
was part of the stern and superstructure –

Four men stripped the last of her metal fittings
in the afternoon. Inquisitive youngsters
were curtly told to leave the shore.

In his office overlooking the harbour,
Mr Bruce Jones of the ship repair firm said
he could not discuss the matter.

'The RNLI did not want it publicised.
I got all my instructions verbally.
I must honour the request.

'It is not uncommon for this to happen.
It would be rather unpleasant
to put a new crew in a disaster boat.'

XIX

I keep seeing them wrestle you into
your trousers and your shirt, and then
you're left alone to be a Nemo to all
and voyaging through earth in
your wood and brass submersible.
How cold you are but no colder in
that sunken death canoe. I think
I shouldn't think of you down there
wizening in the wet and heavy dark,
but it comes to me in the supermarket
when the baker hands me a fresh loaf
and I put my hand between its base
and the bag to feel the heat, the way
I did when you were new-dead, between
the propped-up pillow and your back.
How known that warmth was: my hand
resting there a finite set of times.

XX

Grant them peace, Patron of the sea,
Smith of the winds and rains, from
Gall of salt's final swallow.
Grieve for them, who would save
What sons they could, from
Farrier of storm's hooves.
Grieve for the Ferry's men, Saint
Andrew: these were your sent sons.

DUNDEE DOLDRUMS

(continued)

O empti saile, quhare is the wynd suld blowe
Me to the port, quhar gynneth all my game?
Help, Calyope, and wynd, in Marye name!

JAMES I OF SCOTLAND

23rd Doldrum

Sailors' Graveyard

Eftir, eftir, owre lang eftir
thi stanes an thi banes
                                    o thi shipmaisters' bairns,
sea symbols in saft grey-broon sandstane
    lyk the backs o troot
flakin aff in flinders fae time's lang roastin,
compass rose sheddin petals o direckshun,
three-masters' sails blaan awa beh decades
    lyk a sudden gust,
anchors rustin grains until
    thir hook is no sae prood;
thi stanes that cannae stey, thi voyages
                                    o thi thirteen nemms –

oor fishin faimlies i thi graveyaird's fleet
    ahent Fisher Street, ahent
thi space whaur thi auld bench sat
scrattit wi thi initials o meh sweethert,
seeventeen tae twenty three, murnin furst love as tho
Eh kent thi dool o thi deep's depairtures, thi grane
    o lossin bairn eftir bairn
that keened fae these stanes aa that time
at meh deef back, me sittin wi nac hint
that they werr there, tint i thi dwaum
    o thi sea's deid aa gien up tae
                                    waatir's basest mool,
thi sleech o sea's sheet, thi settle
    o coffin ships, thi galleons gone
                                    amang the gallons,
Monck's plundirers sunk unner, waves fur gravestanes,
    gowd plate and siller lyk clabbydhus in clabber,
        passageweys aa deidmenpends doon whilk
Mona maks mane fur hur crew...

eftir: after; *blaan awa*: blown away; *ahent*: behind; *scrattit*: scratched; *dool*: misery; *tint*: lost; *dwaum*: dream; *mool, sleech*: slime; *clabbydhus in clabbach*: large mussels in mud.

24th Doldrum

Thi Toun as homunculus o us
    supine assa fleh i thi soup,
loose as the soup utsel slops in thi bowl,
Tay as thi broth o a bay; Dundee's airms an legs
    flang oot fur thi oglin,
        wings tae catch thi girnin breeze:

Fluker- and Argyllis-, Sea- and Murray-
thi fower gaitis o thi twa-portit city –
    gait o thi toerag an thi toff,
        thi Worthy and thi Waallace;

nae knackers since thi Shambles
    geed wey tae Commercial St –
did he dress tae thi richt
or thi left? Thi ex-Narrows winna say
tho his politics dae.

Auld Steeple fur a Polyphemic ex-ee
a wad-be keeker-oot fur thi neist Dudley,
Montrose or Monck tae mess uts nest –
thi neist Captain Nemo tae *impune lacessit*.

Thi Toun as oor ain monster, reanimatit
beh a succession o Frankensteins fae
    thi 1540s tae thi V&A.
Is he deid again, and deposit
fae thi cross o thi Law,
    or is he jist haein a wee bit doss?
aa things faa and ur again rebiggit...

lehs: lies; *girnin*: complaining; *gaitis*: streets; *twa-portit*: two-gated; *ee*: eye; *neist*: next; *impune lacessit*: attack with impunity [Latin] (*Nemo me impune lacessit* is the motto of the Order of the Thistle); *doss*: doze; *rebiggit*: rebuilt.

25th Doldrum

> They fairly mak ye work for yir ten and nine.
> MARY BROOKSBANK

Hunkirt wee man in blae skeh blue
sniffin sumthin – son o glue –

aff thi feet o thi cornucopia
on thi Clydesdale Bank: whit hope fur ye,

stottin aff doon thi Murraygate
tae yell at yir pals, nithin blate

as twa beat polis daunner beh.
Nane o yi can meet thi ither's eh

upon an April eftirnoon,
Dundee still a twa toot toon:

thi auld grey coins oot thi Horn o Plenty
gee aff a dust that doits thi tenty.

And thi dragon sez tae thi wee Coffee Tram,
'They fairly see thi wurk-free damned.'

stottin: staggering; *nithin blate*: not at all shy; *eh*: eye; *doits the tenty*: stupefies or puzzles the watchful or cautious.

26th Doldrum

When the ghaists o thi dinged doon
   ur mair real nor thi new-biggit;
when they're nearly mair there as ghaists
   than as yir memory o thum;
when yir dwaums o thi ghaists ur mair real
   nor thi air cut thru the lost stane o thum:
     thi space
                   whaur thi sel maun levitate,
whaur thi legs o memory can hae a hing
   and footer fur a footin
                  and find nane;
whaur thi fisses o thi deid hae seepit back
   intae pub wallpaper, ilka skin cell
haundit tae a blackdeathwaatch beetle, ivry pore o yir ill-
mindit anes
       donatit til
a monamaggot i thi hert's sunkenmoncken aumry –

listen tae thi ghaisties o Dundee
i thi doldrums of eftir-yir-aforelife, street-
singin i thi backies wi nae fronts
crehin tae thi windies wi nae gless, nae fremms,
                          nae waas, nae sterrs

       Eh focht in twa wurld wars
       & Eh'm hung-ry...

   Doon comes the manna fae nae man:
twa jeely pieces wrappit in a page fae *Thi Tully*,
                   Extra Ower Late Extra;
   a thruppenny bit fae nae wifie neither:

       Here ye go –
       awa an dinnae sing ony mair.

dinged doon: knocked down; *hae a hing*: lean from a window to observe or chat; *ilka*: each;
backies: back yards; *jeely pieces*: bread and jam.

27th Doldrum

Tae loup intae nithin
thi haill trenn flehan

intae nocht, intae nicht, intae north
steam wings fauldit an faain

i thi skreik o munelicht
i thi glaik o midnicht

wi Hastur as the Demon o thi Air
and Buster fur an engineer

afore ye hit thi waatir
thi gas lichts' glitter

lyk quaartz in black sand

…

ye thocht ye'd understand –

ye thocht there wiz somethin
tae be understood in Tay's grin.

Thon gap rebrigged huz differed space
fac space: while in ut, beh some grace,

aa's suspendit, naewan's deid,
no yet, nor fur ilka time succeedin:

ilka crossin is the same,
altho thi river's no – time's tamed

and maks a Doldrum fae
disaster, eternity fae this ae dey.

loup: leap; *skreik*: shriek; *glaik*: gleam, glance, trick of the eye; *ae*: single, singular.

28th Doldrum

Fellini fiss oan thi Nummer 73
mune-broch o dehd black herr aroond
yir perfickly medd-upness, fictive Signora o
    thi late fifties tae early seeventies,
bus-pass tae thi Ferry that beh
thi Liz Taylored arc o yir broo
                          shid tak ye tae thi Grand Canal
  or at least thi Dorsoduro, curvin lyk yir spine,
thi bus a vaporetto noo, sliderin
      thru thi decades past
  thi Eastern Necropolis, Diaghilev and Ezra therein,
mascara *maschera* fur thi wintry
festa della nonna in Piazza Santa Margherita,
    an Aperol or an Irn Bru afore ye,
fluttirbeh shades i thi thinnin sun,
                   Peggy Glugginhame
  doon thi Strips o Craigie and up
      past thi *palazzos di iuta*, mooth
a Montalcino o lippie, a Loren-lie calligraphy
    o thi unsaid, thi lang untelt,
        thi niver-comin hame…

Nummer 73: a Dundee bus; *dehd*: dyed; *festa della nonna*: Grandmothers' Day [Italian]; *palazzos di iuta*: jute palaces [Italian].

29th Doldrum

The Fireman's Daughter

Staunin in Broon Street fissin a waa, fissin awa
frae whaur thi Fire Station wiz, and aside ut,
thi hoose o thi heid fireman, and in ut,
   thi heid fireman's dochter.
This bein thi semm sad sandstane waa,
grey unyieldin strips, that wiz
oor vertical mattress: pressin ilk intae ither oan ut, een
tae een,
        mooth oan mooth,
                 breist tae breist –
ivrythin o us on ocht but whit wiz ahent me:
hame's doonhaudin wecht.
                Aa oor lorn subornin
a future owre faur aff that shairly wid
but didnae come.
           Turn and aa's dung doon,
hoose and station, dochter and iver
meetin in this life: the meenut wiz
thi life, timed oot, thi kiss thi mairriage, unbeddit.
Turn and aa's brunt
             i thi years' ships' bombardment. Turn
and Editor Doldrum shows thi cut – no even
thi fiss o sma toun Eurydice fadin intae
hir ackshul life
   lyk the dauphin's fin i thi Tay –
     aa's gane, aa's tint, aa's slaw
       sleight: wiz this yir caird? Naw.
       Wiz this? Naw, that wiznae ut.

doonhaudin: repressive; *lorn*: desire.

30th Doldrum

Snugs

Lament fur the snugz o thi Fcrry,
made tartan corridors fur thi insertion
   o deep-frehd camemberts intae thi baald
and thir wifies, wha cannae help thirsels fae
glaik-govin at thi gowk
                       caucht at his dirty drinkin –
Eh, moi, masel, wi nae taste fur yir widescreen
   fitbaw inferno: eternal wee legs o sinners denehd
aa hope o Heiven beh thi Auld Firm's ticht heuristics.

Thi snell wund blaas thru shoogly swing doors
whaur, thirty year back, we ghaist bairns sat
at thi ghaists o tables, pressin ghaist buttons fur
pints o MacGhaist's, thi nicht thick an bleezin
   wi tales o thae futures we niver did see.

Lament fur yir kneebanes, waarm as stanes
   oan a beach, awaitin Demosthenes Megalostoma;
lament fur yir dwaums o snugs braw as *banyas*,
   Soutar-and-Shanterin wi thi wick an flicker o coals,
holy as thi tongues o sanctit gowks we niver gote tae be
but beh default,
             caucht oot beh
                      thi turnin tide,
Tay's neist indifference aye takkin us beh
   thi semm, jaa-hingin, mum surprehz.

glaik-govin: stupidly staring; *gowk*: fool; *snell*: very cold; *shoogly*: unstable; *bleezin*: blazing
(equally descriptive of a fire or drunken exuberance); *neist*: next; *mum*: silent.

122

31st Doldrum

Cloud City

They didnae even let thum collect aa thae
   white letters aff the frunt o Halleys
      afore they dung ut doon –
sae aff the auld jutemill tuke, hauf-nemmless
   as tho intae air or ether, but insteid ut wiz thi either
      side o or, as in 'either ye cuid knock ut doon, or...',
fur this is Dingutdoondee, sae Halley's awa
   intae the nithin atween Dundonian stars,
comet wove o frore memory, anely tae retour
   i thi wee resurrection o photies, or prophetic thocht
wherein thi haill ghaist o oor toon sall be rebiggit
      hereaboots or oan thi Mune
whichever micht occur least sune:

   Nephelolithogenethlialocheeakokkygia
weavit fae *altocumulonumbnuts nonmutatisdundi* cloods
beh mithers themsels medd o hauf reid herrins' banes
   and hauf noddin horsehair plumes and ponytails
tae snare and terrifeh ony Vicarious Nastyanax
      as cares tae tumble beh.

When uts exiled dwaums bigg mair o a toon
   nor its cooncillors' schemes can ding doon
makkin Alexandrian a herbour that, awauk, 's nae mair
   nor a pelvis o sandstane; recoverin AntiRhodos fae
the thrapple o Tay; swirlin and birlan the Wellgate
   i thi swellachie o thi Ladywell till
Mannahatta is medd o thi Hulltoon, a cathedral raised
anely tae be ruined fur Logie, anniz Erasmian college
   foondit whaur the Ice Rink wiz demolished.

   Thi 45 cinemas sall be refurbished,
   aa departments restored in Draffens,
D.M. Broons, Robertsons, McGills lit beh nicht,
thi Pillars lyk a Moscow kirk fae dernit plans

re-prentit in 3-D
                    as Hôtel Dundide
                              o thi Illuminatit Antarctic
          till Blackness is renewit – meh skale
     as polar memory *palais* fur dole proles' souls:
buiks flap lyk ainguls i thi steep storm o sleepin air
          whaur uts classrooms wull sit.

Nithin in Dundee can neither be
     destroyit nor, lyk tae Detroit, deTroyit eftir aa
since ilka mind here and awa
hauds ut, minds ut,
                    city upon city, nicht beh nicht,
                                        dwaums uts encore,
haunnin ut oan lyk a tuneless ballat, or very like ane epic
     meh hametoon's Homers'll tell ye whaur
the Pola–Cola Bear noo set amang thi stars
wiz furst penntit oanna waa; whaur Glebe Street stude
     back when Paw Broon wiz a young Stobie boy
that syne is Auchenshooglet awa;
                              they'll recite
the genealogy o ivry chipper lyk
                    a lost ship list.

frore: frozen; *retour*: return; *thrapple*: throat; *birlan*: whirling; *swellachie*: whirlpool; *dernit*: hidden; *haunnin ut oan*: handing it on; *ballat*: ballad; *penntit*: painted.

124

EXECUTIVE QUATRAINS /
CAPTAIN, MY CAPTAIN

O what shall I hang on the chamber walls?
And what shall the pictures be that I hang on the walls,
To adorn the burial-house of him I love?

WHITMAN

Executive Quatrains/Captain My Captain

1 *inaugural rain*

Czar Trumpo's tiny hands try to receive
the harlot raindrops: gold as aspen leaves
in fall, they flood his Rushmore of a face –
lachrymal simulacra with a tannic trace.

While Danae once was quickened by that gold
coined by Old Thunder's testes, The Donald
reads omens as critiques, and cannot rearrange:
soon Heaven itself shall know the future must be orange!

*

In an attempt to circumjack terrible times I went to Cork Street in '86
and listened to the acrylic wherein a noiseless petrified spider said
Thinking reeds of Spaceship Earth this is your Captain speaking
in this episode of Captain Beefheart versus the Trump People

> *Flayed fawns squash into*
> *the corner of your eye*
> *as though your head was a pie*
> *and your vision its thumb*

> *They are green and glow on*
> *yellow-fawn snow;*
> *blood makes a pinky smoke*
> *from their Monstromo nostrileros*

> *Wolf minus top hat but*
> *retaining blue cloak, attacks*
> *brown thing on same field of snow:*
> *red sun head reads*

Don Van Vliet is dead and you cannot petition the word with paint
indeed purchasing Green Tom was too much for my bank manager
the snowflakes were like hermit thrushes singing in slow motion
of what really went on in there we only have this recording

2 *the misrule*

As Caligula's horse takes up the reins of power
in his puckered grapefruit of an arse;
as the Capitol's sky responds with a fools' gold shower
and this cul on the Hill expels foul gas;

as his little Goebbels berates the post-soothsayers
from the press room of the Whitened Sepulchre
for numbering the Bacchae in the public squares
on behalf of his dyspraxic sulker;

Spooks of America attend to their Gibberer-in-Chief
while he turns his toxic thumblings down,
suspending his million minions' disbelief
while the horseshit trickles, thin and brown.

*

Language you were always going to tell us what's going on
but you're just going to have to put up with the things we mean
to say with you instead as we claim to be speaking in mansplain English
this is the voice of degenerate art it knows you can hate it Hauptman

> *A volcano attempting to breed*
> *lighter than air geraniums which*
> *are really thin dribble ribbons*
> *expels Lilac Thing with weak heart*
>
> *Lilac Thing falleth biblically over*
> *the mountain, into crisp cream*
> *(whipped and artificial). The ocean*
> *beyond is evergreen/*
>
> *Thin linseed people, as much*
> *as to say 'donkeys' display eyelash*
> *infant, as much as to say 'grow more'*
> *become extract of lilac, orchid*
> *of some brown kind*

Say sound means to be in you to mean and not as backing
means metaphor is what you and not we think with already
in our heads close-walking like to dancing with us when it sings
or parts of the symbol all assemble in each other's body parts

3 *a gowfbaa welcomes a bawbag tae balmoral*

In my short career as Scotland's totey acned moon
I've been bludgeoned tae fuck by mony a rich lizard
and while over the snaa-plugged holes I've flown
I've noted my fellow boneheids' native character:

unless you are the Orange Monarch of Irn Bru Glen,
the Tangerine *Taoiseach* of Clan Orang-utan,
or the Guid Auld Bauld n Cauld Gimperial Gizzard
of aa Blue-Ersed Flehs, you have nothing to fear.

                            *

What is it like this to imagine someone you'll never know
on God's Own Golfball except in language fail and frailing
sailing his coffin trailer upon the High Mojave canvas for sails
those were seven octaves that was his voice becoming whisper

> *They all make people purple*
> *with the cold, naked, swimming*
> *in the hills; they breathe brown*
> *with people in it, purple cloaks*
> *go rage through hills with old*
> *Bootface in them – he's purple too*
>
> *Bootface with blood lips is*
> *a dog's body travelling across snow,*
> *also,*
> *deep blood shadow is his arms*
> *and his blue bow*
> *is a thoughtful doghead transporting*
> *itself into the next field*

128

On the phone down the long draught dead line back to where
the sound of him was all you knew of the at-playing song
pouring like sand from the boot of a radio a dansette it's not
so hot here as it was for him hymning in the topical hothead night

4 *if in doubt, bomb*

Whether travel-bannin, health-denyin, or buildin his Wall,
poor Trumpo can't cut no evil deals at all.
Thank MOAB for a swing at that good ol' death penalty –
just gotta scale its execution up to the planetary.

'Kill the Arctic, drink its oil
Trouble rubble and double the spoils;
Fuck Korea, can't back down –
The world is not a big enough town.'

Although our monsters may count up the ways
to economically kill their millions –
by bombs or gas, famines or climate change,
beneath their nails remains the one vermillion.

'Orbán, Erdogan, Putin, Xi –
These are the guys that think like me.
Grab Le Pen and come what May,
The world is mine to sign away.'

*

To listen as ekphrasis is an act of praise sculpture you need
an ear for armature constructing him like a cure for ghosts
from throat to gland to hide to lash to large eyeball rolling in the dust
attached to a style note clothespeg as though it were attached

> *Captain crept in on a cat*
> *couldn't keep anything back*
> *he swung his aeroplane sleeves*
> *and crayoned the air*

the rest had meanwhile turned
all to cream
(that was why its grin was first to go)

Captain didn't let go
he diddled that crayon to and fro
he made the air a brown stick flow
or would've done
if the painting'd go

To a piano string a star unprepared for snapping its rays
to become a seed head rolling through alphabet soil
orbed in meanings like a magnet that could breathe
gravity in and out as the sun dropped and the moon hopped

5 *strait is the visit*

Trumpo and the Queen enthroned
upon a golden barge
went steaming down the Thames to see
the narwhal called Farage.

'Is that a dick upon his head
or is he pleased to see us?'
'We'd really far prefer it if
you'd cease to yank and knee us.'

'The Earl of Leicester, we recall
took such-like liberties,
but come what may, our stomach's proof
to blandishments like these.'

'I got no guilt, so give me gold
and never mind the plots,
We'll never save South Thanet
if we don't pile on the knots.

'By Margate Sands, I understand
we'll connect our hands in prayer –
But until then, sweet Wall, lala,
all's Mar-a-lago, Leia!'

        *

The high desert for your ocean floor, a shiny trailer for
your lobster casket or nautilus helix because Nemo couldn't dream
for 20,000 lower leagues without repeating himself you had to fare
farther than there were fathers. The other moon that rolls around

> *Hernehead as he led his lilac darling*
> *into the yellow glade of nothingness*
> *like the golden glade of godliness*
>
> *'Here horns flow*
> *and the green can know*
> *the back of the coral's mouth'*
>
> *in his sad down-under-sea*
> *vampyrateuthache voice said*
> *'Here triangles blank-limbed blow blow'*
>
> *and so so on he went*
> *with his pink thing in*
> *her skin skirt*

Tolling against the inside of the mantle arose and filled your ears
with dark and dismantling music it was beautiful as an army
putting down its battle-flags on seeing there was no *thálassa*
and picking up its surfboards except the only army was bones, Bones

6 *golfo de la empatía*

Let Nero rise from his grave, appalled,
his claim to infamy overhauled:
no longer is self-deifying insolence
measured in burnt Romes and screeching violins.

Thanks to a fixation with black sportsmen's knees
distant hurricanes seem a tiny sneeze.
let the new indifference be measured by all:
Puerto Rico, die quiet, Storm Donald clubs a ball.

*

You knew from the inside of childhood that there is no news
in America not scripture: copshows gunsmoke chronicles
soap asylums of the psalms, ads by way of commandments
so the cartoons do for revelation Kid Prodigious you broadcast

These are the creatures kept on a fence:
fat floppy owl with a flounder nose
and Miss Cousin-to-the-Moon.
They were fabulous buddies while
the black moon glowed
and they posed
for their oil photograph.
They were so nice
the light had to creep round them/

Go swimming in chlorinated water
and see what you see by the bottom
of the pool.
Flesh went dog and then came sphinx
the ballerina's head became
the water. The bodies floated up
and ground
there were flowers when she got down

From the bedrock studios of your room while Mother fetched Pepsi,
slid soup beneath the door you carved arks in Clark Ashton Smithstone,
heard if birds are singing then we the people are as birds talking
your sound associates took oversense your letters wrote their ownscapes

7 *der totentango*

Pity the Trumpo, neck-high in swamp
whence even Steve Bannon has fled:
if you once sit down with Satan's Mugwump
you *will* shit yourself with dread.

Spare a gawp for the GOPlites, dingling like berries
clung to Don Dungbeetle's arse –
fearful of uteri, melanin, fairies,
then finding there *is* something worse.

Shall der Totentango circumvent
a waltz with the Daily Stormer?
Dance away the excrement:
Baby put himself in a corner.

Let the squirrel dance with the polecat,
the muskrat with the skunk;
now the Republican frugs with the Fascist
like a hooker must with a drunk.

*

The mess of ages has got into the messages like photons in the photos
our TV eye got stuck on this documentary channel so all it sees is large
unconscious scenery say our bodies are a spacecraft full of soft dials
you've got to tune these better selves had better turn up sooner or louder

> *Looks like some bum's been*
> *burning chopsticks*
> *those who can still swallow will*
> *fly to escape and spread the news*
> *Chinese food's black tonight*
> *and hard to chew/*

> *Big dribble duck*
> *on the dark pond*
> *waves slaver too*

If the aliens came back it would be to listen to the dawn chorus
and maybe a whale or two who knew what it was doing and you
while the presidential cartoon cavalcade drives past in a cloud
of pulverised camel dung from one of the dinosaurs' worser futures

8 *sonetto per trumpo solo*

You may not flip a middle finger;
I may back the ArmaLite.
You may not, moneyless, malinger;
I may tweet my hate-sick shite.

You may not wish to be destroyed;
I may shower food on koi.
You may not believe my boasts,
but I may profit from my post.

I may shoot an elephant
in my invisible pyjamas;
you may not query, point, or hint,
nor interrupt my psychodrama.

I may grope in horrid night;
you may not switch on the light.

*

Caged in renegado cabin not far off Mulholland Drive
in El Valle de Santa Catalina de los Encinos
fed on soya beans and piano for forty days and nights
perched on defunct dust-sucker, Brother Grey-Brown Bird sings

> *Fox in white claws meets dead*
> *spirit thing just leaving its fur*
> *'Hello, must you be going?'*
> *'What would you be knowing?'/*

Here the bad things discuss cloaks
and have a big grin. Fox has caught
a tongue volcano. Stone Head With Ears
is staring, having been
under the yellow yelling ground/

Fox eat creatures
Rabbit lam a lamb
Lilac Thing come out of watcher sun
the more the wolf eats,
the more he gets the ghost
but he eats

Captain Beancult, Drumbotnik be thy sluga although
with heel figurines of clay you trample down our traumas
still your steal of blues is counterspell to Trumpolino's curse
ol' Hole in the Head gangster, hetman of the Go West Horde

9 *memento aurantium*

I am Trumpo's Op-Ed hair –
his follicles have been breached –
I whisper, like a charioteer,
'You can be impeached.'

Some claim I'm made of plastic nets
retrieved from the abyss:
an ancient shrimp within me nests
and whispers, 'You're the pits.'

Some say, instead, I'm Russian straw,
annexed from the Ukraine –
or perhaps, since I flap like his jaw,
I'm just leakage from his brain.

Whichever, whispers this *auriga*,
as his Triumpho staggers along
soon our empty one will roar, 'Eureka,
I'm naked! Et tu, Bouffant?'*

135

*As imPOTUS would not permit
fake Greek to irritate him
(nor pseudo-Latin), this last fit
may not be quite verbatim.

*

The great moment keeps passing as the window of the canvas
closes but is never shut, the run-out grooves run on
but are still in their Zeno phase of the xenochronicity,
that time so outside of time you almost believe it is true

> *Egypt is on our left*
> *Mummy's gone blue*
> *I never saw her before*
> *with her special spider door-*
> *opener. 'This is pig,*
> *he's your father son.'*
> *You're much thinner than*
> *the people I know.*
> *'That's because I've come*
> *to let you go.'/*
>
> *Bend over backwards*
> *and maybe the white thing*
> *won't hit you*

That there is no time inside the great monumomentum,
although you see now that the painting is closed, although
you hear the click of the let's-settle-this-peaceful-like arm;
that the record is both ceased and silent, so you believe

JESUS MARY AND JETSAM 2

Θὰ βρίσκονται ἀκόμη τὰ καϋμένα πουθενά

CAVAFY

Those poor old things must still be around somewhere

(tr. EVANGELOS SACHPEROGLOU)

Verbotentotentanz

3
It's braa when ye're deid
fur aabdy sais
thi lehs that they shid
huv said tae yir fiss.

Thi weemen confess
hoo handsome ye werr,
thi men reminisce
yi were rerr on the terr.

Yir table talk – Christ!
Did naebdy tak notes?
Yir scrievins are prized
lyk cuddies prehz oats.

Yir rep huts a peak
lyk shite huts a fan,
fur nearly a week –
You. Are. The. Man.

Excep fur us losers
wha naebdy read:
we haunt oor auld boozers
as tho we're no dead;

wha lived oor haill lives
like we werenae livin
as hermless as knives
in Cutlery Heaven.

It's braa when ye're deid
fur the time niver passes:
you push up thi weeds,
worms push up yir arses.

If Jesus's Faither
kens ye're broon breid
its hell fur yir leather –
it's braa when ye're deid.

If Jesus's Mither
jist pits in the Wurd
yi fleh back thigither
and sing lyk a burd.

But if there's nae Jesus
jist naethin insteid
on eternity lease us:
it's braa when ye're deid

Helen in the Bardo

(for Helen Kidd)

> Born with a water noose around the heart,
> I hanker for this vast cold cradling.
>
> HELEN KIDD, 'Dunter'

1

No one asks the whale's back if
it wants to be an island, but of all the safe
houses thereon yours was most secure
or so God's operatives mutter through

my meditative heart, still as it were
sat beneath a tree I couldn't name
in that Kidlington stoned back garden dawn
thirty odd years ago, part-larch, half-birch –

all barch according to our voices' potlatch:
were we then too mimsy? If you have to ask.
At least we were prepared for a few years
to silly walk the silly walk. Avatar of Unglish,

of rainbow-socked *karuṇā* after the Tibetan fashion;
Kyōgen non-*sensei*, Mistress of the Unravels;
Anti-Circe in that we began as college bores before
your floating of our circle; blithe spirit leveller:

you danced like Jagger crossed with Tigger.
Kenning galumpher, word-hull's dunter
in the ink-seep's sleep; losers' menagerie manager,
mother of both Kidds and cadence; sussed sustainer

whose soups grew granular as lunar seas so
we could have some more who had forgotten that
we ate then you; lone skater on mind's glass fjords
under memory skies' decades-thick meniscus.

140

2

So that was where I went when I couldn't locate
your funeral, and all your children who'd been put
to bed last night so we could drink our fancy malts
and dance like Morlocks, were now adult,

blond and sensible, older than hadn't we just been?
This millennium's morning had renovated the room
where I'd done *t'ai chi* like an eel in a sock
and told you that I'd taken something bad.

While on the Papil Stone, beneath the Cross-of-Arcs,
the Crane Twins stand in their feather mantle, or
éncheannaigh, enabling the wearer to fly; and pinched
at the key of the arch of their beaks is your head.

Earlier that today I couldn't even find the bowl
in the refurbished Ashmolean, the one
I was always supposed to remember, remember?
Either it was Tang and craquelled celadon

like a tortoise shell made of mutton fat jade, or
of a cello rosin tint interiored with hare's fur glaze –
whichever grail from which we'd drink rice wine
on that future's island where we'd all meet again,

on which instead the church was full of you
not being there. And when the many therapriests
spoke of you it was like a voiceover when
you're so gone that you think the voice is yours.

3

'This is the Whale Eye. Our island, our home. It is
a small whale, wiped by waves, but for us
it is a very important place. Suppose we look away
from the Eye and travel in our imaginations across

the roaring nothingness between the waves.
Can we remember the sort of people who once lived
on a whalefish like this? Let us go very far away.
Let us look and listen very carefully.'

Tibetan prayers like bunting on your coffin,
wicker, naturally, a laundry basket of you,
but with yourself all washed away, mother into
Moomintroll, jokes into *jöklar*, journeyings

across dark waters populous beneath kirk's keel,
fathomed with fathershapes, pews crewed
with your kids eloquent as pirates, all
the poets silenced as stowaways while

sunlight's stick insect legs stalked the walls
and we, ex-chiels and doubled agents, wondered
where your basking spark had gone, that cast control
and all fear out for a few year-long seconds

but knock knock said the vital shark, on the waves'
frosted glass door. Who's there said nobody at all,
who already knew how you, my dear, latterly
and laterally, have been bolted into Bardo:

4

'Attend and I will tell the story of the great fish
Aspidechelone, as it was told in the *Physiologus*,
where the Black Middens stand guard against
the cold sea, in the bookless night that is so long

that the Northfolk sit by their great log fires
and recreate with wordcraft's cunning
and wit's whits the poem of the ponderous fish,
also called Fastitocalon, fierce to seafarers

and fiery-hearted to all men, that monster
unwillingly met on wave, wanderer of ocean's lane,
Jasconius, Imap Umassoursa, Zaratan –
for all that every seafarer supplies another name

none can recognise this rough boulder back,
these raised beach flanks, those sand-dune flukes,

so each imagines they sight an island, and moor
the high-prowed cobles with cables to that fake,

make fast the current-coursers' reins and clamber
onto land. And there I found some herbs to eat,
and a spring of clear water. Then I came across
a fine mare, tied to a *katana* like a post.

We had not been on the curious island long
before it began to quake and tremble:
I was astonished to hear a voice calling me
from underneath the ground...'

karuṇā: compassion [Sanskrit]; *sensei*: teacher [Japanese]; *jöklar*: glaciers [Icelandic]; *katana*:
sword [Japanese].

On Napkins

I am sorry that that the same is not in use amongst us, that I see the Example of in Kings; which is, to change our Napkins at every Service, as they do our plates.

MONTAIGNE, 'Of Experience'

Λευκά Όρη, white mountains;
the babies' knees in sheet peaks;
bergs adrift from the Sea of Counterpane;
shark nosings; collapsible Sydney
Opera Houses; beakless swans
spattered speechless by Montaigne –

'I foul them more than the Germans do
and make but little use either
of Spoon or Fork...' Softly pyramids;
triangular manuscripts, on which
we read each other in
the frank calligraphy of appetite.

I'd wear napkin pyjamas if I could,
and, bibbed to the brows
in crisply ironed origami armour,
arthropod of the dinner table,
I'd insert grub via spork and dribble
wheresoupever I may.

No one knows how
Montaigne's napkins were
folded, so I imagine them
being idly restated in
his hands' 'true language':
now plain, now plesiosaur;

first square, then squinch;
seeking the Platonic napperkin,
first among linens; cottoning on
to the volute of a neck

like the beginnings of
ferns, uncoiling before

the lighted taper on his table
thus rendered juvenescent as
primeval sun, light hitting
the cloth's wedge like
the flank of a white whale
emerging from a frozen strait.

If we could share one meal
he lamenting my Latin, me lying
re his kidney stones,
we would change and we
would change napkins as often as
his perfectly imperfect mind.

Λευκά Όρη (Lefká Óri): White Mountains [Crete].

The Municipal Labyrinth

Harriet takes the money and hands out the clews:
red plastic twine on old spools kept in a wooden rack
by the till; shows the children where to tie their ends.

Edna sells boilings and noodle soup at the second booth.
Everything is still the original cream and green-rimmed tiles,
kept spotless if a little chipped and discoloured by remains.

There's a slight echo in the stairwell of excited voices
from behind the dark wood doors, and the smell
of sweat and disinfectant takes you back to your teens.

'It's the good old seven course unicursal,' Harriet says.
'Square edges – none of your 70s curvers, though it did
get lined with plastic.' 'Orange and avocado,' Edna adds.

'Scratched easy and dirt in the scratches. Awful mess
when we took it down from that "hoof-free" glue.' They tut.
'Now it's back to like it was and the public love it.'

'Single walkers from 7 a.m., schools from 9 – parties of seven,
boys and girls separate.' 'We've had regulars for years,
in and out in fifteen minutes – never found the centre, or so

'they claim, though how they'd miss it...' 'The ones that ask you
for a plan.' 'I say there's postcards of the big mosaic here –
you'll know all about it when you're there.' And the monitor?

'Old Mr Aster can't get round much now, just props up his labrys.'
'They say they'll send a new one but who knows when?'

On Cutlery

The genealogy of cutlery as revealed by each family drawer:
Mother fork, Father knife, Number one soupspoon, Baby teaspoon.
One set of wooden grandparents, spoon and spirtle;
the others steel – fish-slice and ladle. Uncle Breadknife, Aunt Masher.
The crazy cousins Corkscrew, Ally Grater, and that wild one,
Will-o-the-Egg-Whisk. The fish dissectors slept elsewhere
like Arthurian knights in their velvet sarcophagi.
No knife-sharpeners till you're married.

Every kitchen should have a tuna fork, a macaroni knife
and a rinseable spoon. The Blue Raja
could snatch passing birds from the air
and use their feet as forks until they broke.
Lou Macari sliced the machair with a penknife for peat's sake.
Uri Geller sate upon his throne of undulating spoons
and prevented Brexit for a spell.

In our drawer for decades lay the quasi-dental
implements for infants, tampers and trowels
stamped EPNS, as though to lay on a baby's gums
a course of brick teeth. To look down on the blunt,
vertiginous cutlery of childhood is to gaze from
atop a Harpo-sleeved waterfall of dessert spoons at
a deep clear pool of ancient washing up. Old soup bowls
and saucers go back into the fields around earthhouses, where

they form the tectonic plates of Pictland. If you press
your elephantine ear to the whorling stone pits
by Ardestie and Carlungie you can still hear the shrieks.
Listen to the harmonium of the skewers.
Let us not forget the tea strainer, which can be worn
in miniature plastic cocktail sabre duels, or seized to espy
the evidence as might a steampunk fly detective.

Let there be a shout-out here for Crew Cruet, especially Cretan sets,
such as the double-dispensing Mistress of the Labyrinth
shaking one snake for salt and the other serpent for pepper.

Plus a minotaur's head full of mustard. My grandmother had
a china pair in the form of squirrels for Special.
Ratatosk had a bad case of white pepper dandruff.
Ivor Cutler had a briefcase of ivory cutlery
of which he sang as follows:

The fork was narwhal, fifteen foot,
designed for toasting crumpets:
no narwhal gets too near the fire –
the flames alarm the limpets.

The knife was rhino – yes, I know,
you think you'd rather starve.
But as the beast was still attached,
We always let it carve.

The spoon was pygmy mammoth: wee,
just right for soft-boiled eggs;
breakfast was served up soft-boiled trees
for we had giraffes for legs.

Our toothpick was a walrus – blunt,
and apt to rasp and roar,
but worst of all he wouldn't fit
in our ivory cutlery drawer.

Letter to Cath Jenkins

Dear Cathy,

        Here's how the Ferry's been since you left:
the art deco Regal Cinema where I was an usher
and got locked in one night with my girlfriend is now
a car showroom; the Edwardian Post Office
outside which we broke up is now a bar;
the Fire Station and the fire chief's tied cottage
where she grew up is yet another carpark.

Such traces of the civic village we both knew
have been dung doon by the hammer of the profits –
even the gothic United Presbyterian kirk has been
for sixteen years, the Gulistan (a rather fine Indian);
even Woolworths on Brook Street is squatted in
by that barbarian, Mutability. But change itself forgets
before the toun was douce, the thirteen families
went doon to the sea in Baldies and Zulus,
afore we were Prods we were Picts,
and ere we were Papes we were Erse.

And we share a language as vernacular as
their cottages on Fisher Street, now much sought after;
as Sandy Hole Gaelic, which my grandfather heard
as a bairn, like the pipes being practiced, still badly,
in the Burgh Hall, or the Victorian lettering on the YMCA,
or the golden manicule on the glass of the library doors
held open by volunteers.
        The gnocchi in Visocchi's,
where I met Dad for coffee every Saturday
of his last year, still dawn in an Aurora sauce,
the soup of our day is still a moon of minestrone.

That dialect of peh and pastry is spoken yet
in Goodfellow & Stevens: Black Bun, bridie
(baith plenn anes and ingin anes and aa),
butter rolls and perkins, Selkirk bannock and soo's lug,

the placid clock face of Dundee Cake still minuted
in almonds.
        And the river still accepts us aa
in its mile-wide mirror of the upper air – strollers,
waders, Ancient Amphibians, dogs like doges,
sciffiers, yachtpersons, even those who jump
from the roadbridge, anxious, in the words of the song,
'to be weightless again': cold mother, it receives us
all, and rolls us away like time, which its tides
also, exactly, reflect. Much love,
                        Bill

On Brown Paper Bags

As though you were the original rustler,
imagine the tailoring required for
a true brown paper outfit, one you can't
fight your way out of, recalling the roll
attached to the coonter in the Sosh
on Peddie Street: the thunder bang and tear

of it, the grainy tan or 2-D corduroy;
the fashioning by hands extending from
a grey warehouse coat: bags, twists, pokes;
the tin scoop of lentils, sugar, pudding rice,
timpani-alleying paper till the sellotape's
rasp and seal as though making midnight.

Their faces are outlawed by memory,
perched in doo-high darkness, as though
our childhoods were night from five feet up;
as though they were black and white
outside the bubble of our fingers' reach;

were television, comics, cologne
but afar, at source, not here; as though
brown paper was memory being folded,
as though time were a dried thing,
and black tea was text, poured from books.

But now you are appropriately garbed,
let us return as ever to the subject of pies
or indeed bridies, and to their grease,
and contemplate the brown paper bag:
not the bleached bag, that almost seems
to invite the stain which disgusts it;

not carrier bags of plastic or jute,
which we will celebrate elsewhere, but
plain brown paper, healer with vinegar,
best of conveyors, as the Young Lochinvar

151

contains youth, holds bravery, and bears vigour,
so too the brown paper bag with pies.

Were Trigger to swallow Roy Rogers whole,
he could not rival how a bag of brown paper
swallows a roll, itself like a retriever's mouth,
filled in turn with Lorne sausage, or black pudding;
or, roll-less, how it holds just a caramel wafer –
or, if that were not imprudent, two.

Even now I find I still must carry
inspirational brown paper bags around,
preferably in a brown paper bag.
Still I must iron the mottled paper from
the chipper and place it on my writing desk.

Still I imagine placing everything I own
in a separate paper bag. Even now,
I feel the need to source a brown paper bag
large enough to pop over a tenement,
possibly this one, that we all may sleep.

Verbotentotentanz

4

This thing you're in
buttoned up with skin
where does it begin?

And let's not pretend
my fleshy friend
when does it end?

Part one way ticket
part straitjacket
though you could unlock it

I think you'll find
there's no refund
on this underground.

And as for its pith you
admit it's a myth you
can take it with you?

Death Wullie

Here's Death Wullie in
his dungarees o doom
cam tae ding ye doon tae hell
in yir peely-wally room.
In yir cairtie, oan thi trenn,
in thi street or at thi gemm,
aff tae work or gangin hame,
he'll dag n bag ye jist thi semm.

He taks a muckle javelin and
he jabs ye in thi breist
he's the skeleton that maims and shames
at the absence o thi feast.
As he brains you wi his buckct hear
him scream intae yir fiss
'Did ye think ye'd live fur evir
ur ye trehn tae tak thi piss?'

His skull is medd o sandstane
anniz herr is leaves o gress
his nieve is knucklet irin and
thi wurms drap oot his erse.
He's staunin i the Nethergate
distributin black spots
tae aa thi traitrous fuckirs wha
parade whit he's no gote:

oor herts that beat, oor fleesh, our three-
dimensionality;
oor nebs that dreep, oor een that greet,
oor sweet banality.
Wi a peashooter that's pitiless
he bestrides auld Wishart's Airch
passin pestilence tae passersbeh,
Destroy withoot thi Search.

He's yellin 'Hex on Wee Ecks!' and
'Therr is nae hope fur Soapies!'
Though naebiddy can hear him, aa
sall feel his noosey rope as
he hings em fae thi lampies
and flings em i thi Tay
(the Kulchured he defenestrates
fae the nearest V&A).

He mammocks PC Murdoch and
he burns doon ilka Broon.
He sticks a pump up Fat Boab
and ascends thus, beh balloon.
He flochts abune the city wi
his payload, leid-lined conkers,
and renns them doon upon the heids
o auld yins and o younkers.

And then, jist as the final few
creh him Extinction's Prince,
his mither rairs and Dundee's spared –
fur tatties, peas, and mince.

ding ye doon: bring you low; *peely-wally room*: sick-room; *cairtie*: child's cart, usually self-
constructed; *dag*: stab; *blooter*: beat; *keest*: taste; *neive, neb, een*: fist, nose, eyes; *mammock*:
tear into shreds.

NOSTOS

I heard the voice
as I was gazing at the sea trying to make out
a ship they'd sunk there years ago;
it was called '*Thrush*', a small wreck; the masts,
broken, swayed at odd angles deep underwater, like tentacles,
or the memory of dreams, marking the hull:
vague mouth of some huge dead sea-monster
extinguished in the water. Calm spread all around.

GEORGE SEFERIS, 'The Wreck of the Thrush' tr. Edmund Keeley

Cold City

How cold is Cold City? Never quite enough
for its chattering citizens – the men, beefy-faced as
pomegranates; the women, white asparagus:
here it is permanently frost and never snow.

Seeking ancient pockets of the deepest chill,
you find a bridge of old, lobeless buskers
on which music itself sharpens into crystals:
listen quick before your eardrums become paper.

Light from the frozen river daubs the palace's
and the museum's windows as if with cold cream.
In a neighbourhood fogged by the breath
of the long departed, you try to be better but

your saliva has already stuck you to the sugar
icing walls. All tongues will be confiscated
and left hanging by razor gangs of surgeons
who pace the streets in fish-eyed pince-nez.

Only its bronzes are hot to our fingers,
as though posing in saunas, noses dripping
with a salt mineral snot. Naked, one half-rises
from her crouch in a prinkling basin to gaze

out of the courtyard: through its arch, a car;
over its roof, a vennel; at its end, a solid canal;
on it, a boat, and, in its cabin's glass, like a boil
ing oblong of electric marmalade, the sun.

The Sleepers

(Medelhavsmuseet, Stockholm)

We know the terracotta sleepers of the shrines
will never wake again since their removal
from Cyprus's belly to this cold capital
where their heads are like islands through glass.
We know we know too much to let them look
as though they're dreaming: their eyes were once

painted on the clay, wide open to awareness
that the pupil admits more than light; all signs
of seeing rubbed away by fretful centuries.
So now their glabrous brows can shield
neither lids nor lashes, barely bulges for
the orbs that may not flick at myths within.

This one, with a beard bunching like grapes,
dreamless; that one, from Aphrodite's fane,
no matter what reverence may seem to lengthen
her mouth, cannot be confirmed as hierophant
or Herself the Goddess; this one, cap too tight
upon his not-skull's hollow, eyeless but still

not blind. The island sent them all into a dream
of the outside of time, amid the bulls standing
in human bodies, hermaphrodites with lifted arms,
the Goddess whose throne is flanked with sphinxes,
the God who hobbled to the tolling anvil;
sent them to their marriage of foam and copper.

The island, then, a mother with many navels;
those islands about her – peninsulas, promontories,
anteriors – these concentric islands now, navelled
by Gamla Stan: all centred over and over,
the centre of the world found everywhere at once
behind the blank eyes of statues, never asleep,

not dreaming, never to be woken again.

Byron's Mask

for the Venetian *Carnevale*
looked very like the face and hair
of Byron, as though he had
a Lord Byron's head-shaped onion
for a head, and could simply pull
skin after skin off, each revealing
a slightly smaller Lord Byron's head
until the final tiny head, still
with Byron's features perfectly picked out
like a Patryushka Giovanni Don-doll
and, when this last shallot of Lordy Gordon
was shed, as though he would walk around
with no head at all. In fact
it was in this manner that he wrote all his best poems.

Follow Me

Studs in the prostitute's shoe
print ΑΚΟΛΟΥΘΕΙ in
the compacted Attic dust
and, whatever we think
of text or lust, we do.

Fish-fight at the Basilica Cisterns

The toll of living voices like irregular bells in
the domes of thin red bricks which diminish
in concentric astroids causes the fish to fight.
Their long grey bodies, eager for blindness,
slide over each other in the umber shallows:
they are like pigeons in a long-buried piazza;
they break the surface of having been forgotten
the way the historically dead break the surface
of fiction, and are for a moment real to us again.
There is a slither of light along their scales,
as though in the eyes of secretive lovers –
it is the same light which sits in the pupils
of the coins, which the fish pass over as though
they had no value in their eagerness to feel
the words nibble at the lice which line their backs.
Columns recede into the darkness as though
they were the echoes, as though echoes could
hold up the city, as though the voices
could cause the fish to begin their sluggish
metamorphosis, from scales then feathers back
to nails and eyes and tongues, coins
dropping from their goggling faces, erupting
from their drying throats in cornucopia
as they resume their robes and their roles
in the city, columns pushing through like tulips
into the astonished air, so that even the sun
blinks, unable to tell if it is day or night.

The Dream of the Airport: *pakama*: plaid sash or wrap [Thai].

The Dream of the Airport

The car hire company bestows upon you the great gift
of abandoning you to the airport overnight. Returned
to the eternal striplights of your early travels,
you wrap your head in the checkered *pakama*, place
the green Ethiopian Airways eyemask on your face,
and insert the orange earplugs which can't quite block
out the music of The Continuity – that shuffling of the less
lucky travellers, banging of trays as their diminished
possessions are scanned, ping and pronouncement
of the missing's names by the same old siren. How many
decades have you been passed through here without
ever leaving home? Try escaping into your recurrent dream:
the one about an airport. Then it's four. Abandon sleep
to walk directly through the dream of the airport:
its labyrinth as one bright uncomplicating hall.
Your Minotaur passes, long horns carved with lists,
memoranda, minutiae of the dates he fears. His horns
score both walls at once, his hooves click and chip
this marble. Here's your chance to miss tomorrow
in its role as The Next Episode, to lose the need
for such times to pass, that dumb urgency. Go out
into the night's cool breezes: be glad the bus
which will return you to your place in the action
has not yet arrived. Look up: there are still no birds,
no stars have been allocated to you. You forget, but
this is the hour at which your father died. The night
is like a charcoal horse pacing in its ash paddock –
it chafes itself away as it walks. Walk back into
the long departure hall and pass among the pissed-off
officials, the ecstatic sleepers. We are already within
Asclepius's temple: look, at the opposite end
she's still asleep, the woman you must travel with.
The furniture of your luggage surrounds her like a room
with no walls. She is sleeping in public: we are all
sleeping in public, together, sleeping in public together
forever. Go to her and rewind yourself in the shawl
and pray, your head to her head. The lights keep burning.
Go to her and dream about the airport in the night.

Pagomenos

Crete is cold for Easter not their Easter.
Cloud sits like concrete roof slabs on the hills
while justified by snow the White Mountains
raise pyramids behind, icebergs that stain

ruddy as the Holy Weeks' evenings queue
to kill their Christs in order. The fields are full
of irises, white like discarded veronicas;

great thrashing clumps of dark leaved lilies
then the fleshy white spout, the nozzle
of turmeric; later furlings emerge straight up
under olive trees like light green peppers.

Malotíra lines the fences, yellow dabs on sage;
and pockets of *papoúles*, which Chaucer knew
as vetch, crowd out kitchen gardens with
their soft fishhooks of tendril, ear and petal –

we eat those with Cos squeezed with lemon
from the trees we planted for lost fathers;

gather oranges from blossom-bursting branches
to press into two tiny tumblers of Spring tears,
and cannot light the timber Tassos saws us
till we scavenge for kindling in laybys' cowps

on the road to Alíkambos where the little chapel
backs onto the rock face like a walk-in freezer
in which Pagomenos painted his masterpieces
on every surface like a hang of carcasses.

They'll open it for Paskha but we'll be gone.
Light will come, *phos* from Iraklio from Athens
from Jerusalem, and Xristós will again be *Anésti*.

The light will fall on the defaced Agios Mamas
and on the Papás jabbing Jesus in the eye
explaining in broken French and rural Cretan
how this frozen barrel can cradle the Kosmos.

malotíra (μαλοτήρα): ironwort, used for 'mountain tea'; papoúles (παπούλες): peashoots; phos
(φως): light; Xristos Anésti (Χριστός Ανέστη): Christ is risen, statement said at Paskha, or
Orthodox Easter, the reply being 'Alithos Anésti (Άλιμος Ανέστη): Indeed he is risen; Papás
(Παπάς): priest.

Portokáli

The stickiness of juice is everywhere like light
on the oranges' attendants: olivewood board
and knife; blue plastic cup with its pointed dome
of radial serrations that requires a name
more exact than 'press'. How many shapes
we live with as nameless as how many
of these hills' hundred varieties of *hórta*.

Amid which the picking: stalked pairs that won't
be separated; the cutting into and interiors,
pipless, twin elder suns that hiss their essence,
zest from the *zestí*; you press with increasing force –
first the hand, you even try the chin – then
the whole gentle weight of the upper body
as the lover presses upon the breastbone.

Sound of the gussies releasing below, un-
certain yield, meagre or an excess of giving;
spent halves piling in a sort of soft ossuary,
all skull-tops and no jaws. Fill and clink
small glasses that deserve a silver tray
to set them down on; four lips touching glass,
reluctant at this sharpness before such sweetness –

as hot, almost, as raw garlic; then, thirst as eagerness,
the animal finally given permission to drink.

horta (χόρτα): wild green; *zestí* (ζεστί): heat; *gussies*: segments of an orange [Scots].

Zone

As you descend into the amphitheatre of water
formed by the first or last inlet of Almirou Bay
where a mountain rivulet debouches its layer
of absolute cold and absolute freshness
on top of the sea's warm brackishness, so that
the sheep pause there to drink on their way
to be milked, a zone that now your ankles,
now your shins, and now your thighs,
are realising roofs this entire inlet,
your attention is still focussed on the actors:
fishing boats mostly entering stage left
from behind the breakwater, exiting the harbour
past the indifferent *psarotavérna*, then letting
their lines go, their nets out to gather
the little fishes like diacritics escaped from verse
in shoals around your feet; your eyes shifting
between these and the backdrop of mountains
painted pink and cinnamon behind Rethimno
as the cold belt or girdle or band or gorget
rises as you advance, till the almost waveless
translucence collars you with a cool noose
and your feet lose the bottom, and your body
finds its axle, wanting to swing you till
you float in those few inches of still freezing water,
ears filling and tuning to its translation
of both aboveness and below: the narrative
of powerboats and swimmers' languid chatter,
the *vrathini vólta* of sightseers along the causeway
to the brine-stung chapel of Agios Oudeis, ceases
to grip your attention, catharsis-schmatharsis,
you starfish, you sunfish, are held momentarily
above the general element, and fix your gaze
upon that colour the far waves emulate,
the one you hear the Greeks never had a need to name.

psarotavérna (ψαροταβέρνα): fish restaurant; *vrathini vólta* (βραδινή βόλτα): evening stroll.

167

How to Drink Ellenikós Kafés in Emprosneros

Up early always, increasingly so
as his eyes' auld lenses calcified, denying
enough of yesterday's light to soothe the mind
and let him sleep through dawn, my father sits
and drinks *kafés* with Apostolos,
who would've risen earlier still
to see to the sheep he'd bought
as austerity bit. Neither sharing
more than a word of each other's tongue
they drink their *kafédhes* in the freshness
before cicadas, tops of the White Mountains
cloudless, the occasional rooster hoarse.
'He slurped it, and when it was done,
he poured his water in and swirled it,
and drank the grounds, and that's how you do it.'
I've never seen anyone do this
but let it stand, the two dead men
swirling the water and drinking the grounds
in the hush before the heat wakes up.

Ellenikos kafés, kafédhes (Ελληνικός καφές, καφέδες): Greek coffee, coffees.

Kombolói

The first beads preceded all worries:
blue Adriatic ceramic on slender leather,
a souvenir of the island I couldn't thread
our link to from the walking sticks

carved with 'Κερκήρα' and old men's heads
in my grandfather's black box of a pitch-
painted potting shed. In Corfu Town
I understood my mother understood

something of this script, let its words
punctuate her speech like the click of beads,
miniatures of the far sounds of snooker
on my grandmother's black and white set,

or the knock of bowls at Barnhill, back
in the same decade that got Click Clacks
banned for concussing my cousins; in
the Year of the Bellbottom and the Chopper

they split and flew apart across the old
linoleum, its patterns as lost as mosaics
beneath memory's dirt. That unsettled that,
until the new set, bought for Dad's birthday,

with the mulberry staff and Sharples hairnet
of a Sfakian gentleman brigand, smiled over
and put away in the polite drawer: black
as bakelite on a silver chain. No amber

tears from dead pines, not even faturan's
dust of those tears, blended with mastika
and frankincense, no coral mothered
these cold berries on their Marley's links,

suitable for a northern concern. No scented
rosary, no diurnal round of prayer, just
the occasional mnemonic – names of aunts
and uncles, old school friends, now lost.

I turn them not quite Greek-like, half-
hidden, like glimpses of a stranger's spine
as they bend over to attend to their child,
and can never stop following their fall.

Κερκήρα (Kerkyra): Corfu.

Maroudianá

Each ratcheting-up cicada morning,
in the stomach-like *plateía*
of the village just below,
the rasping van man begins
to advertise with megaphone
and pre-recorded lyra
his glut-hoard of glorious *laxánika*.

In the long green outside room
of vine and patio, I wait
for my daughter to wake up
as my father would wait for me
in his greater garden of the past
with all the urgency of ageing
and nothing more to say than *kaliméra*.

I watch through walnut, jasmine, and
the swaying of tendrils in descent
from the canopy, leaf mottle leaf with shade
in the roll of still early air
up the valley, as birds squeeze through
the blurred lozenges of light
cast on table, chair, and patio,

translating them to *trapézi*,
to *karékla*, and *avlí*, and see
down in their *kípos* and our garden
the stone that is not curled
like a cat sleeping, and does
not dream of a cat, curled
like a sleeping stone.

What we have to say to each other
will not wait for understanding.

plateía (πλατεία): square; *lyra* (λύρα): Cretan lyre; *laxaniká* (λαχανικά): vegetables; *kaliméra*
(καλημέρα): good morning; *trapézi* (τραπέζι): table; *karékla* (καρέκλα): chair; *avlí* (αυλή): yard;
kípos (κήπος): garden.

Whose English Is It Anyway?

How we speak is who we are
if you hear what I mean,
but is English without anguish,
the way Westminster dreams?

If the language was London
it's a giant cut-glass shard,
but if English is an engine
then it's thrumming to depart.

Let's head through the Heptarchy –
the nations that we were –
where speech is like cryptography
and the code begins *oo arr...*

Have mercy on us, Mercia
where Big Geoff Hill once played
where Shakespeare's vowels too were shaped
alongside those of Slade.

Here's stone-head Brigantia
she's blocking Ro-ome's gutta –
a goddess for the Geordies
but what, pet, would she utta

in to-ones like wor Cheryl
on mattas of state,
like once the Jocks aal leave wuh
let's follow – why wait?

Here is the language
nearin the border,
beginnin bewilderment,
Scots and disorder...

Gin the ingyne rins on Anglo
wi a Saxon heid o steam
then Furst Class is a quango
whaur they don't know *what* we mean...

'Oh Darling, look, there's Ber-whick,'
a Norman type remarks:
'They're still at war with Russia,
but then so are we – what larks!'

The issue's comprehension
but not of what we say,
the issue's why should 45
declare *we waant awa*

– Thon rhyme's agley twixt mooth an lug
the wey a politician's shrug
isnae solemn like a Vow:
whit noo, Paw Broon, eh? What now?

Faur ur we noo and fit is at soond?
– The Doric: at spik o baith quinie an loon
Aiberdeen wey, an twal mile roon:
the nor-east o someplace – mebbe the Moon.

O please stoap the trenn – Eh waant tae get aff;
meh leid is disgracefuhl, meh heid's gaein saft.
Tho this virus crehd 'Inglis' mutates beh thi mile,
it's no spoken beh money, it's no spoken beh ile.

Faur owre, faur owre, fae New Aiberdour,
whaur Trump pleys gowf wi an affy shower
o bankers an lairdies an gangsters an Tories
wha aa unnerstaun: *own the words, own the story.*

gin: if; *ingyne*: genius, invention; *agley*: astray; *lug*: ear; *Paw Broon*: Gordon Brown, issuer of
'The Vow' during the purdah period of the Independence Referendum; *quinie and loon*: young
woman and man [North-east Scots, or, Doric]; *leid*: language; *ile*: oil.

BAD MAKAR

Gude readar, veip and murne this mortal lyif,
As did the vyise philosophour heraclite;
And thou sal laucht for scorne recreatyfe,
As faste as did the prudent democrite.
Ane murnit for pite, the tother leucht in dispite,
Quhen thai beheld this varldis vanite:
Bot var thai nou on lyue, i mocht veil dyit
That thai vald laucht and veip our misire.

Verses after PHILIREMO FREGOSO, *The Complaynt of Scotlande*

Tyne Valley Section

From Blaydon to Shields, from Hull to Dundee,
the passengers ask us: where can the North be?
We appear to be in it, or are we at sea?
Is it rivers or mines, is it you or just me?

1

How do you know you're in the North?
the gurnard ask us, beyond the bar at the mouth
of the Tyne, lying in the disturbed silt
and making expansive gestures like to shrugs.

Is this north of you yet? the lobster enquires,
slinging a shotgun over one shoulder
as it exits the quadrille in the Assembly Creels,
and heads for the ghost of a carpark.

2

Legionary, lay your shield
upon the Tyne's broad breast
as a roof for the river where
a crossing might be effected,

here where the tribes have set a border
between what it is to be northern
and that which may instead be known.
Let a print be lifted from that design

which the spear point and the arrow etched,
where rust and the engraver worm
cross-hatched, and hang it for a sail
so those curators of provincial allegory,

the kittiwakes, might inspect its motifs,
long obscured by the impatience of the tide,
and discuss with the magpies and the crows
history's habit of not looking properly.

3

See kindly Father Tyne assist
in the delivery of contraband
by jabbing the exciseman's arse
with his municipal trident.

The gulls cry that we must not think
of that which makes you think,
that there be softnesses and warmths
somewhere south of the heart.

O where is the boatman, my bonny hinny,
and where's the boatman from if not from here?
Here's the Roman keelman from Iraq
or from Yemen – is that coal, is that corn?

Is this home, are we free?

4

See where the old bridge goes down
in a flood unknown to Noah
and unremarked by its successors
while here they burn the enclosures

that the Town Moor be not improved
in the way the motorway has enhanced
our understanding of the Brutal.
At three on a Sunday morning in November

the Gateshead end collapses
and the mercer and the milliner
and the cheesemonger and the shoemaker
go down in a swirl of timber,

tar and planks and noosing ropes,
where chare and channel are made one,
while two surgeons, Bayles and Gibson,
cut through the Ponteland turnpike.

At five the northern arch falls in
and Charnley's bookshop's stock
is distributed to our scaly readers
while mass trespass fills the Moor.

Bewick mans a boat that oars it
to save those on the central arch.
Wooden roofs flipped to cobles
and crewed by dogs and cats

are carried the miles to Jarrow Slake.
While the Assizes forgives the burgesses
to the tune of two milch cows each
to graze in perpetuity, a cradle

floats past a ship off South Shields,
and up by Bywell horses are brought
into the kirk: they save themselves
by clutching the pews with faithful teeth.

   5
Steer north past the two lighthouses
who gossip at the bar, and the couples lying
in the sand fully clothed, as though
still standing up, but felled by a cone.

The river is broken by itself,
it is a crop of herring fins.

Like a crocheted shroud your wake
flows past the woman with a white dog
dangling from her wrist by its jaw:
it will hang there forever.

The river is a nomad who never leaves,
a migration to where it already is.

You pass the wake for Farne's final puffin
in its open coffin. It removes a sand-eel

like a tab from its beak, and remarks,
'I ain't gonna work on Lindisfarne no more.'

*The river has already forgotten
your keel and the cut of your oar.*

*

*From Hull to Dundee – does this boat have a bar?
where the Forfarshire met with Big Harcar
the puffins advise us we're wrecked and must sink,
but, Purser, dilate: is there time for a drink?*

North of the Book

1
Cuthbert's cloud crypt is barely blue-flecked.
Beneath it, rapt, his bestial elect
witness the bay as a sunken boat
in which the sea-fowl gospels float.

2
Prior Puffin / arranges fish
upon his profane / palate's dish.

Sister Otter / won't insist
but the bliss of water / is like a kiss.

Brother Crow / can't allow
that a bird might know / how to bow.

Father Gull / holds Bible School
for a fresh lamb's skull / and a crab in a pool.

Mother Whale / dives to foil
the foolish sail / and saves her oil.

Deacon Dolphin / sings descant
to the shoal's cold hymn / in greed's ascent.

Sacristan Seal / wrack his stained glass
ecstatic, reels / in the tidal mass.

Hermit Crab / with trembling claws
grabs scuttled garb / and, ragged, withdraws.

Abbess Cod / knows the abyss
is as close to God / as the white cloud is.

Abbot Herring / in a habit of silver
and a crowd of uncaring / is a harp that shivers.

Venerable Bee / levitates
while her harebell history / reverberates.

Saint Snail / can't explain
but his pilgrim trail / is a glittering stain.

   3

Northumberland's casket of hills
encloses the holy corruptibles.
North of the book the page is born
from vellum sand and tide's return.

The Calotype

(Edinburgh, 1840)

     'Earth's shadows fly'

Here they all are, all four, as though they had lived,
with Burns the grand old man, frail and serene,
but sharing that something round the brows with Byron –
that says they will never be forgiven.
His juniors still look young, though slow exposure
has made Keats waver and obscured the lines
written through his brows by Rome. The real surprise
is Shelley being there at all – that closure
he imposed post-drowning left the muses hopeless.
It must have been the chance to meet with Brewster,
transposer of his vision into glass,
who prints their likeness now upon the future.
They almost laugh that luck's kaleidoscope
has caught them gazing at us as we pass.

To a Ploughman

(falsetto)

Oi, vigorous but wrang Big You,
warld-straddlin addlet Man wi Ploo,
thon wiz meh nest ye jist ran thru
    and blew tae chaff –
jist tak a thocht tae whit ye do,
    and then fuck aff.

Tho Eh micht anely be a moose,
Eh'm still entitlet tae a hoose
thru Naichur's will – tho you've nae use
    fur it or me,
could we no strike some kinna truce?
    Lea me meh lea!

Ye've been this wey wi hedge an holt –
aa pizen, scotch, and eisen gold –
fae ilka final hole we bolt
    moose, burd, an bee:
nae wunner Yirth is in revolt,
    as you'll sune see.

Her coral, coals, and iles ye spile
fae Ayr tae Zetland ye defile
whit geed ye bield, this Pestert Isle,
    thru whim crehd need:
thi Fiend himsel fae you resiles
    de-Helled beh greed.

Let loose on aathin, Lucifer
sall neither moose nor mannie spare
till'iz cloots bestride baith hemispheres
    wi flemm or flude –
when aa ur hameless, then, ma fiere,
    wull you be prood?

lea me: leave me; *pizen*: poison; *eisen*: desire; *ilk*: each; *bield*: shelter; *crehd*: called; *cloots*:
hooves; *flemm* or *flude*: flame or flood; *fiere*: companion.

The Parliaments of Birds

(before the 2014 Scottish Independence Referendum)

go says the crow
stay says the jay

aye says the magpie
naw says the daw

they're bluffin says the puffin
all news is fake nods the corncrake

when says the wren
noo says the doo

what's the rush asks the thrush
God save ye says the mavie

surly and shirky grumbles the turkey
all troubles unlocked claims the bubblyjock

what is the harm, again? wonders the ptarmigan
sic labour'll fail ye says the capercaillie

ungrateful peasants sneers the pheasant
a flu on both houses curses the grouses

You wastrels cries the kestrel
they'll baulk says the hawk

let them loose cries the goose
get tae fuck yells the duck

little shits shout the tits
ye're affy says the chaffie

who'll hug ye asks the speuggie
the way is narrow says the sparrow

it grows dark says the lark
be tenty says the lintie

we'll thole it says the houlet
at a pinch says the finch

Showing Sharon Olds the Carcasses in St Andrews

> Sausages is the boys
>
> TOMMY LORNE

Cheek made me do it after finding us
sharing the minibus

from the golf hotel to the poetry festival:
after the small talk of Fifesplaining, how

its rauchle tongue was embodied in
a dancing descent by crawsteppery

from orange Dutch pantile
to the Englishry of pan loaf tones;

the frothy moustache of the milk bar,
the madness of the mad mill sale,

that led me to Mitchell's on Market Street,
the old window onto their hanging room,

where the carcasses dripped onto sawdust.
Husks of meat and rib flipped vertical

as though bipedal, or heavy garments
we might wear, as I talked her through

hough and the puddings, why dumpling?
the stovies, the skirlie, the haggising;

the slicing of our sausages, their boy-ness
qua Jimmy Logan, qua Tommy Lorne;

our minstrelsy of game and gammon,
our dialects of meal and dripping;

the long coagulations
and maturing of the meat.

Kirsty Wark on Broughty Ferry Beach, Or, An Indy Ref Ode

...a single reality – a' a'e oo' –
O' ... love and pity and fear;
A seamless garment o' music and thought...

HUGH MACDIARMID,
'The Seamless Garment'

Turned oan meh telly – it wiz jist as Eh feared
they wur filmin *Newsnicht* oan thi Phibbie picr.
Ootside meh windae, tho Eh wiznae there,
thi debate went oan, lyk Eh didnae care.
Kirsty telt us aa whit's whit
while affstage drinkers yelled, 'Ye're shit!'
Yesseers and Nawists mindit thir lines
while Broughty Castle did 'sublime':
a pillar o glimmer i thi Dundee dark,
glimpsed lyk the wame o a grecht white shark.
Sprats i thi waater and spats oan thi land –
sma fare fae afar till ye understand,
if whaur ye live is wha ye are
We'll mebbe laive but we'll no gang far.
If wha ye are's no whaur ye live
we wullna tak, we choose tae give –
Freedom's an idea tae share:
we breathe it here, noo inhale there.
Baith 'if's are true or amphibians fib
we're England's ither and its sib
(– exactly hoo they comprehend
this poem's leid as wierd-pretend).
Eh wiznae there, Eh wiz doon sooth
whaur Eh pit breid in mch bairnie's mooth.
Nor wiz Eh oot o Scotland, naw:
ilkane cairries thir ain snaw,
thir ain, thir native airt: its nicht;
Tay's mornin slab o platinum licht.
When Eh luked at thon weel-kent crood
(and heard thae hecklers, hauf-oan dudes),
saw Cox and Marra, Andy and Dylan,

Eh wiz there tae, and sae, Gode willin
(no Westminster, Brussels, NATO or ocht
o thae roguies wha think a nation is bocht),
come Aye or Naw Dundee will be
come Friday forenoon, a polity
composed o pehs and comics, yes,
as much inclined tae blast as bless,
but democratic tae the bane
sae come whitiver, aa at ane –
'Aa ae oo' MacDiarmid said:
let's greet the future as unread.

windae: window; *affstage*: offstage; *Yesseers and Nawists*: Yes and No voters; *wame*: belly; *sma*: small; *laive*: leave; *wullna*: will not; *tak*: take; *ither*: other; *breid*: bread; *bairnie*: child; *ilkane*: each one; *airt*: territory; *weel-kent*: well-well-known; *bane*: bone.

188

Explaining Irn Bru to the English

(after the 2015 General Election)

As the jaws of Scotland swing at the Swing
like a creaky pub-sign in a Jekyllish wind;
as Scottish Labour hide oan a nithin, the oatless ask:
what is Irn Bru, really? Is it safe, really?

Is it Presbyterian perspiration? Is it liquid rust?
Is it produced by an irony brewery, really?
How do you girder a loin? How do you
guard your enamel or your porcelain?

It is the sippoleth, slipping down like sandpaper;
it tastes of mechanically retrieved bubblegum
the dog consumed, producing a Montgolfier arse balloon.
The glass slipper version ate through the sole.

It's différance in a tumbler. It's indifference in a tumbler,
The carbonated faddomer of all hangovers, electoral
and other. Too teuch for orthography, it is an elixir
that would tak the lacquer aff the truth.

Drink this, it says, the transmogrifier of English
into pish, and thirst nae mair for thistle milk
or Islington. This is the Aperol of the North,
the Harpic of the Glens. Oor A&E is your A&E.

The Farewell to Jim Murphy (et al)

Noo Big Jim Murphy's hyne awa
Labour can mebbe see the baa
dernt beh'iz heid fae ane and aa
    baith North and Sooth:
ye cannae defend the weak and the sma
    wi yir fit in yir mooth.

Twa national '-isms' sweep the board
lyk curlin besoms – but wan chord
oan the UK's ukelele's heard:
    Auld Smurfie's Theme,
tho there's mair tae oor vote than Jimbo's wurd
    it's a piper's dream.

Fur UKIP's cap winna cross the Tweed,
nor fit the thochts in Scotland's heid:
the independence that we need
    is frae sic chains
as Tories forge fae fear – sic dreid
    's whit we're against.

There's fascists loose in Albion, aye,
and Alba tae, frae Duns tae Skye
wee tartan bampots' harnies scry
    but thon's no why
we hoyed oot Jim's weel-fingert pie –
    we're trehin tae try.

Wha thinks thir norm equates tae 'Brit'
assigns transparency tae it:
thir ethos, lyk thir accent, 's fit
    fur global use –
no tae agree's tae loss yir wits:
    don't be obtuse.

But wha votes fur hope and no fur hype
wad loup thi turf o stereotype,
Westminster's weskit we aa maun flype,
    weel stitched wi lehs –
furst past the bastards and the clypes
    is no oor prize.

Lehs aboot Trident, penshuns, tax;
lehs aboot doactirs n Devo Max;
lehs aboot frackin – jist frickin rclax:
    the UK's hip
don't need replacin – let Goldman Sachs
    steer Britain's ship.

But we dinna waant austerity,
we'd like tae plant the Liberty Tree
in Embro *and* in London, see:
    wc aa maun spiel
this Hadrian's Waa o no bein rcal,
    sae, Jim, farewecl!

PS
And bye bye Kezia, in casc ya feel
left oot: as Scottish Lehbur reels
fae shattirt promise tae raa deal
    ut's boond tae burn
thru leaders lyk chippers dae tattie peel –
    and niver learn...

hyne awa: gone, at a distance; *baa*: ball; *dernt beh*: hidden by; *dreid*: dread; *bampots*: headstrong idiots; *harnies*: brains; *wekit*: waistcoat; *clypes*: tell-tales; *speil*: climb; *raa*: raw; *chipper*: chip shop.

To a Rat

Ye dirty, fleet-fit, canny craitur,
as feechy as a muckle slater,
ye fleg us sune, and fleece us later –
   oor hairy sib;
we baith came frae ae skrymmory pater
   and shared a crib.

Ye gnaa thru waas and pipes and wires,
oor mires o refuse you admire,
oor pizen jist maks you perspire:
   Exec o grime!
The human race? – time tae retire,
   you won, lang syne.

Ye brocht the Black Death wi yir fleas
and every city tae its knees
sae you could rax wi greater ease
   oor juicy thrapples –
in Eden, tae, received pair Eve's
   discairdit apple.

Tho yir bairns oor baudrins claut fur sport,
tho yir marras we trap, it's us that's caught:
tho Gode smites aa, yet twa cavort
   upon the Ark –
when Ararat became its port,
   plague disembarked.

'Contagion', yir ghaistly banners displayed
on thon Hamelin-abandonin Rat's Crusade:
owre ivry hame and ilk arcade
   they flap lyk bats,
but hoo can we claim that *you* invade
   when we spreid – lyk rats?

We'd chew the Mune richt oot the lift,
regard the Kosmos as oor gift,
squaat in this Yirth and wulna shift
    nor clean oor nest –
richt thru the ozone it has niffed:
    we are the Pest.

craitur: creature; *feechy*: germ-ridden; *slater*: woodlouse; *fleg*: frighten; *skrymmory*: monstrous; *gnaa*: gnaw; *rax*: reach; *thrapples*: throats; *pair*: poor; *baudrins*: cat; *claut*: sink claws into; *marra*: mate; *rat-rhymes*: doggerel.

Bad Makar McGonagalliana

1 *The Resurrection of William McGonagall*

Wha's thon lang rapscallion, plankin oan a wall –
Issut Lowry, Mary Shelley, or Phantasterix the Gaul?
Oh no, it is Oor Wullie McFrankengonagall!

Resurrect um wi a hunnert and fufty thoosan volts:
ane fur each Dundonian fae Desperate Dan tae dolts!
Fur he lacks in kulchur like a vulture's short o feathirs when it moults.

This wad be a joab fur Doactir Kengo Kumastein
(plus a wee bolt fae the Storm Fiend alichtin richt on time) –
a pause...

          a piece o piss!

               Applause:

                    it rhymes! It rhymes!

– Come aa ye media mavens fae James Cameron tae John Craven!
Get yir Keyhole Kates on! Catch this bardie struck beh levin
afore or eftir he strangles ye, or at least while he's still ravin...

Come interview the zombie bard on whit he thinks o New Dundee
And is he oor new Makar? (Since he's deid he shid be free.)

2 *McGonagall and the Burns Statue*

> 'I will ever remember the day I walked in the Burns' procession in Highland
> costume with the manuscript of the Burns Statue poem in my hand, which
> I willingly would have read had I been permitted, but no! when I made the
> attempt for the third time, to get onto the platform, I was told by police to
> go away, just the same as if I had been a dog.'

It wiz ever thus fur yir Dundonian bardie
be they behappit in kilt or cardie:
it's easier a Cooncillor's ee tae meet
gin ye scrieve a letter aboot dog's jobbies i the street,
whereas the polis haud versifiers in keen regard
as anarchic shits fur whom life shid be hard.

As statuary few o us amoont tae a bust
and maist lig hermless in the dust,
but fur McGonagall there maun be an exception
and, tho he couldnae quite go the full equestrian,
could ye no afford, O Cooncillors, in bronze ootben Blackness Skale,
wir ain wee Ahab, Musashi-style, atap the Tay Whale?

But whit wiz written re Heaven, the rich and the camel,
Is jist as true o lucre, and poets, and yir sea-goin mammals.

3 *McGonagall as a Dog*

Gin McGonagall was Buddhist, no a temperencial Prod,
Whit wid he re-begood as, beh the Laa o Michty Sod?

Thi *Logie Physiologus* lists oor local bestiary
Fae bee-moths tint in autumn mists tae fauna foond at sea.

Fae thi murderous bear wha picknickers caa Jezza o Camperdoon
Tae craiturs neither cats not curs fae craters oan the Mune.

Nor elephants o thi Ferry Road, nor zeuglodons o Tay –
Nane o these fae fleas tae toads sall oor bardie's sowel convey.

McGonaghoul requires a hoose o true unsullied fleesh
Nor chuckie hen nor platypus micht be thon speerit's niche.

Fur wallabies or wallie dugs or walruses he scorns
Fur Wulliam's ghaist ut tuts and shrugs and wullna be reborn

But as a hoond he'll reassemble – sae his ticket's clippit:
His neb's a-cauld, his shanks a-tremble; he's Billy MacKenzie's whippet!

4 *McGonagall and the Baxter Park Pavilion*

O beauteous Italianate pavilion in Baxter's Park
Most marvellous to be seen, except when it is dark!
Though perhaps a bat could detect it with its high-pitched cheeps
While it traverses the daddy long legs-ridden nocturnal deeps.

(I should clarify that 'it' would be the bat, and not the Baxter Pavilion,
Which if it could fly at night would be a pavilion in a million.)
When you opened on the 9th of September in 1863
Thirty thousand Dundonians came for you to see.

Men marched in white aprons while wearing red bonnets
looking like French revolutionary waiters to the eyes of this sonnet.
Too late for Mary Shelley, who'd bided with the Baxters in South Baffin Street,
named for where leviathans were butchered by our brave Whaling fleet.

Though perhaps Marxist types would claim, for all the Baxters' acts of charity,
their exploitation of their workforce worse than mere Arctic-set barbarity.
(I myself am loath to judge these two profitable pursuits between
especially as the lines of my sonnet are now, monstrously, sixteen.)

5 *Ode tae Yet Anither Dundee Railway Station*

O beautiful new Dundee Railway Station
for which they should have added, as Ringo advises, an eighth day to Creation,
tho who 'they' are is akin to a knotty theological question
concerning the 'sons of God',* which rather lies outside the frame of the famous
        sticksman's suggestion –
unless it's the Etruscans, who passed an eight day week on
to the Romans, granting them just that little longer to get thir freak on –
something Dun-lovin-fundonians micht appreciate mair than you,
ye big bendy gless banana descendit on us as tho tae spite the EU.

For like the bairns o thae sons of God wha ligged wi the dochters of men
ye're neither hake nor drake, nor are you but nor ben.
Hauf chuff chuff station an hauf yet anither bluidy hotel
fur the prayed-fur kulchur rush – tho this wan cannae spell –
fae 'Sleeperz' tae the V n A,
tho but a pace, is a demographic league away.

And you are less lovely, let's face it,
than the splendid Italianate then Gothic constructions yir shabby predecessor
        replaceit.
For if there's one thing Dundee Cooncil likes mair than a guid deal
it's a deal that lets them knoack doon historic buildins as weel.

196

But of this as of aesthetic style you are wholly unkennan
the way that folk don't really know who the best drummer in The Beatles is,
        according to John Lennon,†
or God or the Etruscans or the need for Renationalisation –
who cares while there's a crap hotel humping Dundee Station?

* Genesis 6:1-4
† Actually attrib. to Jasper Carrot

6 *Address to the Girders*

O beautiful railway girders, which bridge the still Victorian Tay,
so broad and strong and even:
who could have prophesied you would inspire one day
Irn Bru Yum Yums for sale in Goodfellow & Steven's?
A bakey orange marvel of the present day,
Which for just 95p in new money can be taken away!

O girders, which so beautifully bridge the unrustable Tay
How I wish you delivered teapots to McGonagall each day,
Teapots the size of bathtubs wherein he could disport and play
with the whalefish and the seal-people and the spratlings of the Tay,
and serve them and me Spicy Red Chai frae Braithewaite's changeless urns
and thae Yum Yums for which even drooned fowks yearns!

Though gradually wir fleesh would tak on the colour o Trumpo or United
and wir teeth dissolve tae bridge stumps, still, aa wad be delighted!

7 *Broughty Ferry Blackout*

'Twas on the terrifying evening of the 15th of October
An occasion which nae rational man 'ud dare tae face while sober
That the current failed an hour afore I'd intendit tae go drinkin
And, as I headit through the darkened streets, this occurrence set me thinkin.

Maist thocht the lecky wiz knocked oot beh a traffic accident
But whit if thon bump wiz Donald Trump and done wi bad intent?
In his maisterplan tae *untergang* the West End o Dundee
He'd first release the Storm Fiend then bring Europe tae its knees.

But whit, ye ask, 's a Storm Fiend, and why shid we care a fig?
– This is the monster wha destroyed the former railway brig,
Accoardin tae McGonagall and he shid shairly ken
Since alane o us foregaithered here, he wiz alehv back then.

First the hated latest bridge and next the crossins at the Forth
Then the hapless tapless tooers wad topple richt across the North.
And noo the Fiend lang pinioned deep ablow the River Tay
Shauks aff uts psychic chains that like dreh tangle drap away.

At liberty tae chose its form it opts fur platypus –
It is not oors tae reason why as it consumes a bus
Tho the passengers protest they shid get aff at Strips o Craigie
The Storm Fiend squirts oot feechy milk, unpasteurised and plaguey.

Noo the trippin pus o the platypus shall faa on ilka pletty
And ilka hard man shall be heard tae girn a wee 'Oo, Betty!'
Uts pizened claa will swaat the Laa and sweep the police away
While the meek look on like meerkats fae Balgay Observatory.

The anely thing tae save us is that Yin tae Yang o power:
The doggerel verse o auld Dundee that in its broadsheets cowers.
Though apocalyptic platypuses dae demonic dumps
Mere bathos micht remodulate The Donald's Final Trump.

Sae Dundee's Makar, in The Ship, shall beard the platypus
And defeat it wi McGonagall's (adaptit) blunderfuss:
'The stronger we oor electricity substations Dundee builds,
The less chance there is o bein monotremetously killed.'

8 *Address to the Dundee V&A*

Bilbao, Paree, Thatlondon, thon Hull –
o aa the braa toons that tourists could visit
why pick on Dundee? It's duller than Mull
and the hame o the Broons – plus, whaur the hell is it?
    Pit a daud o V&A in wir DNA
    and let's see whit Dundee can dae.
(And gee the Laa Hull monument a Prince Albert beh the way.)

Zenimalism for the zenimals!
Lemonalism for the Jif Lemon Tree!
Municipalism fur wir new principles!
Hing-em-fae-a-lampie-ism fur the auld kleptocracy!

Let's hae a kulchural kouplet, tae prove we're no aa zoomers:
   skate like a Pingu, strike like a puma
   build the V&A like a Kengo Kuma...
Geez anither, fur Eh feel we grow less snidey:
   the V&A is lookin tidy
   lit by nicht like a silver bridie.

Hi ho, drinkers in the Waalnut Lounge, or ye
   wha in Mennie's snack on nosh
wi mebbe a wee OVD n coke:
why no inhale an ingin bridie or
   a plenn ane wi a whack o squash
inna tearoom that's no only bespoke
      but pretty V&A n oak?
   Then spend yir penny backin Scotch
   design beh Rennie Mackintosh!

Let's hear whit we'd clamour fur inna Wunderkammer –
Somethin mair nor the history o the peh
via an incredible edible Land o Cakes Visit-it-n-deh-orama!

Eh'd waant tae ken fae Kengo, micht it be whit we creh 'humour'
or is there ony truth tae the scurrilous rumour
(be it wondrous story or spurious conjecture)
that, deep in noo-borassic laboratories,
the V&A is growein back the architecture
o demolished Victorian and Albertine Dundee?

See, were it up tae me, or in meh gift,
a new Auld Wellgate and Overgate wad descend fae the lift,
also a new spire fur the Royal Excheenge, weavit softsift
frae thon maist precious metal, Nostalgium,
signifehin that the Kengo-dom o Kuma hud indeed come –
basically a new spine fur Dei Donum
biggit fae seevin whale vertebrae sellt affa barra

threidit thru wi the sangs o Brooksbank and o Marra
lyk therr wiz literally nae thimorra.

Gee us a museum that's no jist a mirror but a witness
tae the toun o whale ile, liberty, and sweetness,
tae uts weavers and uts worthies that noo are wede away,
let the canny and uncanny deid speak within oor V&A.

levin: lightning; *behappit*: wearing; *polis*: police; *lig*: lie; *maun*: must; *re-begood*: began again;
tint: lost; *neb*: nose; *bided*: stayed; *ootben*: outside; *lecky*: electricity; *alehv*: alive; *ablow*: below;
tangle: seaweed; *trippin pus*: unhappy face; *pletty*: platform or outside landing on a tenement;
daud: a lump of something; *zoomer*: hopeless type; *ingin*: onion; *borassic*: pennyless; *ile*: oil.

Ode to the USS *Discovery*

(Season One)

Dundonian is Klingon tae
sci-fi's prosthetic lugs:
oor Neutral Zone's the River Tay,
oor history is shrugs.

Here *Discovery* first sailed its heroes
tae the pole if no the stars:
fur Shackleton and Scott, twa year o
pack ice n packs o cards.

Oor ship's a widden star marooned
wi jist wan pairt tae play:
hoo ye wance bestrode McMurdo Soond,
noo upstage the V&A!

Taysiders dinnae starry trek
tae hit the synthohol,
hae rammies oan thi holodeck –
sic splores wid sune appal.

See, Arthur Clarke ate his jeely pieces
oan the deck o *Discovery*,
developin Space Odyssean theses
as it sat in a London quay.

While Scotty inventit Klingon speech
wi Henry Higginsian ease:
as tho Pig Latin ate a peach –
ut's braid as Dundonese.

Tho Captain Lorca's war is focht
wi tardigrades and lehs,
Michael Burnham's logic's taucht
in Vulcan – and thi Hegh.

Oor Dundee bugs could easy kerry
ships tae ither quadrants:
forkietaillies fae thi Ferry
caa the Mune their bodhran.

The Hulltoon's horniegolochs hae
a wamefu o duende;
clipshears o Kirkton aft display
a sense that space is bendy.

Know Kelpiens ur kelpie men
wi hermless dulse fur manes;
beh'iz creh o 'Aye an Ayrab', ken
T'Kuvma's Jim McLean.

Jist waatch thon show thru Dundee's een
tae ken uts growth and form:
baith Marra and Roddenberry dreamed
o a warld that begins thi morn.

lugs: ears; *widden*: wooden; *rammies, splores*: fights, delinquent adventures; *jelly pieces*: jam
sandwiches; *daured*: dared; *the Hegh*: the High School, Dundee; *kerry*: carry; *forkietaillies,
horniegolochs, clipshears*: earwigs and similar insects; *wamefu*: belly-full; *kelpie*: horse spirit,
said to haunt streams; *hermless*: harmless; *dulse*: seaweed; *Ayrab*: Dundee United supporter;
growth and form: *On Growth and Form* (1917), the most influential publication of the biologist
D'Arcy Thompson, was written in Dundee; *the morn*: tomorrow.

The Couthier

(On the 200th anniversary of The Courier & Advertiser*)*

Twa hunnert year o fermin news
And Kaiser Thomson's fousty views:
pit Dixon Hawke in chairge o crime,
and Dundee's trams wid rin on time.

The Craigie Gollum's lang syne photics
delicht idolatrous devotees;
while uncouth youth in druggy dorts
are nemmed in sook-toothed court reports.

A broth o bonny illustrations
mind Greetin Teeny o hur station:
see Brechin at Beeching's ex-line's end
lie gutted like *The People's Friend.*

Still, dog's mess, drains, and Bill and Bun
are Girny Jock's ehdea o fun;
while Draffens' ads sell weemen's knickers
tae meenisters (nae priests, nae vicars).

The Couthier kens wir quotidian sins –
it's mair parochial than yir skin;
ye'd rather no get that excitit?
treh Dundee versus Dundee United.

The Couthier kens we're cultural flakes –
Nae book reviews i the Land o Cakes,
but The Sportin Post's on sale, nae leh,
afore thi pea i thi whussle's dreh.

Collect yir tokens fur a peh;
check the Deaths in case ye've dehd.
Ye huv? Well, that explains the smell.
Nae probs – *The Tully*'s sellt in Hell.

fermin: farming; *dorts*: ill-humours; *greetin*: weeping or constantly miserable; *ehdea*: idea;
dehd: died.

Undeed

(On the Tay Road Bridge's 50th anniversary)

When Eh wiz fehv, Eternity
wiz mair than jist a stane
laid in St Peter's Kirkyaird, since
it bideit in oor name:

Dundee, the Toon undeean as
broon sandstane shairly was,
fae Annfield Row past Blackness Skale
the causie sang oor cause –

in sannies, segs, green buses, trams,
tae Fifies ower thi Tay,
things and thir ghaists in harmony
cuid niver gang agley.

Thi leerie lichters Eh cuid mind
Dad said Eh niver saw;
thi Overgate as wiz, aa biz,
cuid niver gang awa.

The Caledon, the jute mills, Scott's,
whaur Granda stude, wool-gradin
in a snaa o fleece, as though time's lease
wiz endlessly Arcadian;

tho Timex ticked, aa Time wiz fixed,
its ilka oor recurrin;
tho NCR rung up the bill,
the future's note wiz foreign.

And naewan deed and nane werr killt
and hearses aa ran late
until the New Road Brig wiz built
connectin us tae Fate.

And Fate uts fiss wiz concrete and
uts manner ut wiz Brutal:
thi seik and auld sank in uts foonds
and much wiz foond inutile.

Fae Newtyle til the Mill o Mains,
fae Monifieth til Gowrie,
Dundee hitched tae Modernity,
and destruction wiz uts dowry.

fehv: five; *causie*: pavement; *sannies*: sandshoes; *Fifies*: ferry boats travelling across the Tay
before the opening of the Road Bridge; *gang agley*: go wrong; *leerie lichters*: workers who lit the
streetlights; *seik*: sick.

Mastercannibal

The Denfiends and thi clan o Bean
baith hud ae ugsome mission:
tae eat aa Scotia, fat or lean,
in a cook-aff competition.

Thi Denfiends bideit beh Monikie,
thi Beans beh Ballantrae:
wan liked tae sup oan Fowk-a-leekie,
wan munched Man fricassee.

Thir contest wiz baith comprehensive
and, cuisine-wise, a stretch –
thi ingredients, tho inexpensive,
cuid be a pain tae fetch.

Thi thrie estates, fae nyaff tae laird,
wi ilka ane ae dish,
thrie different weys maun be prepared
(thi clergy coonts as fish).

Thi Beans began wi Broth MacBeth
a sort of cullage skink
but steeped in bluid and biled tae death –
thi newt ehz clogged thir sink.

Thi Denfiends trehd John Knoxtail soup
but thi keest wiz unca werish:
dreh Calvin croutons, brimstane gloop –
yir parish, parched, wid perish.

The Beans cooked Connery confit
in a nesht o shumwan'sh hair,
anna terrine wha's sheen wiz medd complete
beh thi spleen o Logie Baird.

The Denfiends favoured finger food –
we presume Dyte Livingstone's;
thir Slessor sliders luked dead good;
Brude's bridies, overdone.

Ane barbecued Rabbie wi Fergusson fritters
inna greasy bardic freh;
thi tither geed ye literary skitters
wi Sir Walter Scottage peh.

Ane served a Parcel o Rogues ragout
wi a dhansak o Dundas;
thi tither's chilli con Darnley blew
thi madrigals oot yir arse.

Thi ashets struck thi board as fast
as Crocketts cuid be spatched,
as Grassic Gibbon's giblets hashed,
or Naomi's limbs detached:

Chic Murray Kiev inna bunnet because
his entrance shidna be cauld;
braised Nesbitt brains in Rab C sauce
laid oan a heidband's fauld;

Scotch oeufs de Mary Queen o Scots,
in a lochan o hur gravy;
fresh Para Handy hough in pots;
a Hume-elette o Davie;

wee Lulu in a goulash – aw!
Mock Chop MaGreegor – service!
Sir Alex haggised in a baw –
but noo baith teams luked nervous...

Thi Denfiends hud few pastry skills,
and Sawney feart desserts –
besides, they werr rinnin short on kills,
while Scotland grew alert...

Thir John Broon broonies'd scunner Vic,
lyk thir sponge wi Gilfillan fillin;
while thir Reverend Thomas Spottit Dick
wad find few puntirs willin.

While thi hooves o thi militia scuffed
thir wey tae Desperate Den,
King Duncan doughnuts n Plum McDuff
wiz scoffed beh cannibal men.

And while, thir flintlocks cocked, they moshed
at thi entrance tae thon antre,
a battered Macintosh wiz noshed
wi anthropophagic banter.

Thi order geean, whit they were seean
wad stow a stervin soo,
fur boady pairts, in ilka airt,
werr prinklin inna stew;

werr prinklin, sizzlin, steamin – cooked,
or in man-marinades:
thi wabbit sodgers luked n puked
and fired aff enfilades.

They shucked thi Beans wi baignets fixed,
wi cordite choked thi cave;
thi Denfiends wi thir dennir mixed,
an but wan bairn wiz saved.

O hur latter life ye micht huv heard:
she entered politics,
whaur, haund tae myth, they eat oor words
till truth itsel is sick.

But whit thi people, unappalled,
wad ken, fur Scotland's sake,
is wha's oor Maistercannibal –
results, eftir this break…

ugsome: unpleasant; *cullage*: testicles; *werish, wersh*: bitter; *ashets*: plates; *feart*: feared; *antre*: cave; *stow a…soo*: sicken a sow; *airt*: direction; *prinklin*: lightly boiling; *wabbit*: unwell.

Owed to Groucho's

(On the record store's 40th anniversary)

I'd never go into any second-hand record store
that would have me as a customer –
and you never did: always raising a bootpolish brow
at wannabes from kaftans to leathers:
you kent we were aa really still in our blazers.

Outside of a dog, a second-hand record store
is a boy's best friend – inside of a dog
it's too dark to make out the scratchmarks
on the vinyl. O vinyl: black hole in a cardboard sleeve,
you swallowed our hormones, dosh, and years.

Time flies like an arrow, fruit flies prefer
a second-hand record store: for forty year,
weirdos, creeps, and fowk fae the Ferry –
fur singles wi their middies oot or thae parvenus, CDs –
we hing aroond you, wee Harpos, mute wi joy.

(Hidden run-off stanzas in memoriam Alastair Brodie)

Hullo, must you be goin? Ach, Breeks,
we haurdly kent ye. Wolfman T. Driftwood:
Prog Deacon, Punk Worthy, Emperor Penguin
Biscuit of the Perth Road, oor scabby kneecaps clack
thir bane clappers thegither and toll in dreid

o follaein you doon thi rin-aff groove
tae feechy and unfunky quietus…

Remains of Doggerland

In Doggerland the sunken trees
bear filthy rotten fruit,
and mammoths float in slimy herds
to chew on fossil roots.
The hipbones of Neanderthals,
the sopping hides of Picts,
collide in dogged frottage though
the North Sea has them licked.

O Doggerland beyond the strand,
you Eurobridge that sank,
you link gone lank where King Log planned
to break the Dogger Bank:
you're anti-this and anti-that
and pre-diluvian –
though doggerfish don't love les chats
they're poissons sans a plan.

Your drowned, unsound, and shrivelled heads
still circle sodden hearths
of coprolithic hill-fortlets
and wiggle lugs in wrath.
The princely corpses crawl from wrecks
that nosedive from the waves
and feudalise the fungoid crabs
that scavenge in their graves.

O Doggerland between us like
Pierre between his peers,
from beers to fears your pilgrims hike –
let jellyfishmen steer
your anti-history fist of a ship
against the flowing stream:
you doggers' dinner of the rich
who let them misdemean.

The admiral of Doggerland,
split shot wound round his feet,
with razor-shell dividers plots
to resurrect his fleet,
and raise the ruins, rocks and roads,
the time that land forgot,
the politics improved by woad,
the opposite of thought.

O Doggerland, beneath us all
but not too low to stoop
you soup of gloop where Ned Ludd stalled
the Euro's loop de loop.
You're anti-regs and pro the dregs
of sub-humanity,
the doggerheads who'd bite the legs
of children lost at sea

Rogues Reparcelled

Βρεκεκεκὲξ κοὰξ κοάξ

ARISTOPHANES

1 *(After Burns, and for Ian Duhig)*

Fareweel tae aa oor island's fame,
fareweel oor claims tae glory;
Democracy lives but in name,
for Parliament's a story.
Noo saccharine and hollow speech
demeans a Premier's station,
demarking BoJo's pinchcock reach –
sic an arse tae prorogue aa oor nations!

But sic a guile for mony years,
gained Empire's greedy wages,
and is wrocht noo by a gang o fieres,
Late Capital's bluff sages.
Tho Eton Rifles we disdained,
secure in Labour's mission;
but Eton's gamesmanship's oor bane –
sic a farce tae prorogue aa oor nations!

Auld Éire lang has seen the play
whaur Tories strut but sell us,
and Scotland sune must brak away
tho Tories tut and tell us.
For wi this shower we must not cower,
but mak oor declaration –
the UK's soul is bought and sold,
sic a curse tae prorogue aa oor nations!

sic: such; *sune*: soon.

212

2 *(After Byron, and for Andy Jackson)*

Let's no more go proroguing
    so late into September
though Theresa May's still voguing,
    her memory's but an ember.

For the Johnson is unsheathed,
    and, while Cummings rears his crest,
no Parliament can breathe,
    nor Kuenssberg ken her rest.

Though the Brexit toads are croaking,
    and it soon is Halloween,
let's no more go proroguing
    while BoJo moons the Queen!

The Fall of Brexitopolis

This is the way the empire ends.
The proud nose shall be rubbed in its own hallucinatory piss.
The pony shall be rent in the temple
and the chlorinated dollar carried into the place
of the Holy of Moliest.
Chickens shall speak in tongues in the seats of power
while their teeth are treasured as charms against
the coming of plagues or nurses.
The roughly asleep shall be bayoneted where they lie
to save on bullets for the flat of foot.
Like the tides there shall be an amnesty on bodkins,
and then a redistribution.
Where there is plenty we shall restore rationing.
Where there is home we shall bring deportation.
Johnny shall be as a foreigner whether
he remembers me or not.
The bee shall be placed on trial for the pollution of bonuses.
The ear of corn shall be deafened,
the eye of the needle quite put out.
The sick shall queue to die, their trolleys
nose to tail on the orbital motorways.
The Old Preventibles,
cholera, the pox, rickets, tuberculosis,
shall be released from the laboratories:
collect them all now.
The articulated lorry shall not rest in the ruined nave.
The chorister shall not be listened to with great care.
Also the pea shall be removed from the whistle
and taken to a secure jar.
The ornamental pond shall be filled with ornaments.
The antique shall be tat
and the masterpiece shall not be all that.
The arts shall be done better by my six year old.
Facts shall be the wrong sort, and statistics a poor show.
The Sciences shall be an absolute shower.
Vendors of gin and cupcakes shall take up residence
in the former libraries and shall style themselves

Artisans of Utopia.
The Unity of the Kingdom shall be preserved
by the biting of rum-soaked bullets, a satterlee saw,
and the tarring of stumps.
There shall be a general pickling in the provinces.
Barristers shall be mistaken for baristas,
barrators for orators.
Prejudice, citing precedent, shall be postjudice.
Righteousness shall be called on as a substitute
in the eighty-fifth minute.
The Golden Calves shall be set up in the Own Goals
while the referees are being hamstrung in the tunnels.
Trees shall be netted to defend them from birdsong.
Migratory geese shall be shooed from the Capitol.
Plastic shall be forced down the throats of swans
and, should they wash up on our shores, whalefish.
Nanny shall stockpile Zopiclone and Cyanide
for the coming of Naptime.
The last poet swinging from the last lamppost
shall switch off the final streetlight, whereupon
the Senate shall assassinate each other in order of eminence
till only those too incompetent to stab themselves shall remain.
The self-elected emperor shall then divest himself of his last invisible cloak
and, casting it ahead of him into the absence of a fray,
shall lose himself where the lack of fighting is thickest.

Gunlandia

There should be guns in the restrooms
in every cistern, taped there, so my brothers
don't have to wander school canteens
with their dicks in their hands; guns in
the toilet bowls and sinks seen foreshortened
through clean water; guns dispensing soap
slugs and guns in the water supply
instead of water lakes of guns or at least
on-tap bullets; at table pistol pepperpots
and assault cellars plus lots of gunword
play we won't be able to hear over lunch
with guns instead of cutlery, guns
that fire forkheads and slicing bullets –
spoon your gun soup with an empty magazine –
and guns instead of newspapers or news,
just print the legend along their barrels;
guns instead of cars trains aviation ships
firing us wherever we want to go so
we arrive ready for burial, and guns in funeral
parlours – the priests and mourners don't
need words they just take out their grief on
near-bulletproof coffins; and guns instead
of telescopes firing our eyes at the Moon,
a small squeeze for a gun, a giant recoil
for all gunkind; instead of scalpels guns
at the dentists, pop this gunshield in
as the gunbell sounds the boxers have
special squeezebox guns their gloves can handle;
the referees have guns for all the players
who take the kneecap while in the killing fields
steers instead of horns have howitzers, in
the dead trees gunbirds greet the dawn
with fusillades of gunsong as we wake up
and smell the cordite pills cabinets replaced
with pillboxes the cure will be fired directly
into our brains, which, having been
spattered on the walls of kinder

gartens, libraries, galleries anywhere
we need to keep the peace, will be replaced
in our open carry skull-holsters with something
small but, at close range, effective.

The Nine Trades Welcome You to the City of Refuge

> Our stays here and days here
> Are very Short and Brittle
> They short are, goes swifter
> Then does a Weavers shuttle.
>
> *Lockit Book of the Dundee Weavers*, 1771

The Baxter will bake you a bridie, my bride,
my Mary of all the monsters that dream,
to bind the flesh of the bridegroom fast
all mingled with fragments of shot between.

Then the Cordiner will cut out two soles, my son,
and sew shoes since your pilgrimage is done –
such a shame you should walk to our city unshod
where the Turk was paraded in King Crispin's shade.

And the Skinner gie a glove for the hand that you lost
to cutlass or crime or the snow on the hill
so you'll think of its scuttle like a soft-backed crab,
a shuttle between all the threads in our mill.

The Tailor will stitch up the cloth you'll be clad in
since eternity also has sumptuary laws,
and his statutes still tell us *na wemen sall weir*
na dresses abune their estait except houris.

Then the Bonnetmaker caps you wi a toorie, my boy,
all black with the Indies' best indigo, too,
for it's up wi the bunnets o Bonnie Dundee
since all who pay their fees shall be free.

And the Flesher shall strike you a calf with his axe
on Commercial Street, so it falls to its knees
blinded by blood where the Shambles once stood
for you are all braw lads if dusty of feet.

Let the Hammermen cunningly craft you a gun
of the fishtail design or the old lemon butt
and fashion you both the hauberk bold
and the bullet that shall pierce it.

Then the Webster will weave you a shroud sae fine
as muslin from Mosul, or Gaza's old gauze;
the cutty sark shall be your sign
that your bairns have been swaddled in some future's cause.

And the Dyer will print out your ends and your means
inking his press with gall of the oak
listing your numbers if rarely your names
and sealing the news in his lockit book.

Il Futuro

(after a painting by Leon Morrocco)

So here is how it was, the future, after all:
an orange boat, beached – it's the business, ours,
how family is business: the catch under parasols

hanging on a wall in Visocchi's, the Ferry's
café still, where Dad and I came to discuss
the business of his last year – and it's the son,

Leon, not decades-dead Alberto, who paints
this boatie, 'Futuro', balanced somehow on keel,
gunwale's curve like a mouthful of good grin,

cabin like a Guston steam robot head. Three tables are
atilt before it, fishtails toward us, scales blinter
or catch in the white cloth so they don't slide

off, purple stranded jellyfish of shade off right
a bluish dog contemplates only to mirror
the black fish/propeller arrangement off left.

What is it not exactly in the middle, over the soft
crab's head pillow, that the Picasso patriarch,
assured and sailor-striped, is holding up,

that the pink vase puts its handle on its waist
base to regard, that's not a giant fried egg?
It's hot enough to fry one, that orange,

which only the scale as distance and the glass
keeps from gut-stinking out our ritual,
little window tables on Gray Street's little world,

with exactly how *oíkos* oscillates
between our knowing and its *nómos*: all ology
as loss, the law as that pertaining across

220

any border, frame, or finality we find ourselves up
against. This canvas should blow open the room,
be sail-broad, a blaze of coastline calling us,

'Here, here is your *futuro*, boys, fillet, steak
and roe – don't you want it? Fried
or grilled, girls? Buy it while it's fresh!'

Oíkos (οἶκος): family, household, firm [Greek]; *nómos* (νόμος): law [Greek].

Dirt Bath

As the junior starlings howk
at our tussocky lawns
a sparrow gives itself a dirt bath
in the flowerless verge
just dry enough for it
to fluster and fling a crater
into momentary being.

I glance back a minute later
and half a dozen are there
wriggling and fluffing, winnowing
dirt to dust the colour of their wings
flying in the fine powder
of speuggie-shaped hollows

as though they laid
new eggs, half-earth, half-air –
then they're gone
as though that was how
Spring might be accomplished.

The Giantess

(after Leonora Carrington)

I failed to see a theme was not a thing
you wrote but lived for decades failing
you and all our generations of estranged
Catholics, cousins, the Toogood girls, coughing
like geese in their black-roofed caravans
and dying on the fairs' great circuit of the years,
while all I wanted was how to be a father
but kept losing the single hair
that would lead to my patriarch's beard.

Choosing instead the flotilla around your feet
of whalers and submarines, mechanical
but all-remembering pachyderms, parading from
that inner port you shooshed me for super
imposing on the very pattern of a father,
while the hair, grey and glinty, kinked through
an invisible hedge, and drew me past
a panting gruel of flesh still in
its can of ballad armour.

How I abandoned you and that childhood
of tales I promised and childishly supposed
required no time to make, for my own hurt
and acquiescence in the great men's game.
How it twanged in the burn that flows
over grimy golden wool,
and I lost it in the lichen,
in the heather's etymologies,
I lost it in a hipbone of ice.

Are you stronger than you're angry or just both
at the burning ball we rolled beneath your feet
before you couldn't stand it any more,
giantess of wheat still working out
how to cradle the boiling crystal egg?

Years ago I could hear you calling from
years from now: on the other side of life
there was something you couldn't find either,
so you called out your stranger's name.

NOTES

Fathership Glosa (13)

'He was of respectable parentage and suffered from pronounced hypo-chondria, having the delusion that his posterior…was encased in glass. One day the doctor…ordered him to be seated for a medical examination …the doctor forcibly knocked him into a chair and at the moment of impact had arranged for his assistant to smash a pane of glass on the hearthstone…' (George M. Martin, *Dundee Worthies*, 1934)

Balgay Hill (23)

The Reverend George Gilfillan was a prominent Dundee-based preacher, editor, and poet, who supported the work of William McGonagall among other working-class writers.

The Three Flies (32)

The *Mona*, a lifeboat from Broughty Ferry, capsized in a storm with the loss of its crew on December 8th 1959 while answering a distress call. General Monck, having sacked Dundee in 1651, saw his fleet lost with its crews and its booty in a storm in the Firth of Tay. The 'Storm Fiend' is mentioned by McGonagall in his poem 'The Tay Bridge Disaster' about the collapse of the bridge on the 28th December 1879 in a great storm with the loss of passengers and crew on the train crossing at the time.

An Exotic Dream of Leonora Carrington (70)

Alebrijes are brightly painted chimeric figures made in Mexico from papier-mâché or copal wood. The term is a nonsense word coined by their inventor, Pedro Linares, from a feverish dream in which he first encountered them.

Teatro Orfeon (71)

'Pulque, neutle in Nahuatl, has a strong odour and high alcoholic content. Its patron was the god Ome Tochtli, "Two Rabbit". In view of its calorific value, adults were only allowed one drink, and drunken-ness was prohibited because the excess of pulque would make people fall under the influence of the Cenzon Totochtin or Four Hundred Rabbits, which meant losing control and becoming aggressive and violent' (Museo Nacional de Antropología, Mexico City)

The Antikythera mechanism is an ancient Greek analogue computer used to predict eclipses and astronomical positions; the Tōnalpōhualli is a type of Aztec calendar; the Phaistos disc is a Minoan artefact which may record a hymn to the Sun.

The Wreck of the Fathership (93)
The italicised passages in this sequence consist of found material reworked from accounts of the Mona Disaster on the Friends of the Dundee City Archives website. This material was written or compiled by Iain D. McIntosh, and I acknowledge here the generosity of both Iain D. McIntosh and Dundee City Archives in allowing me to use this valuable historic resource in this way.

24th Doldrum (116)
'The town is divided into four principal streets, which we may suppose a human body stretched on its back, with its arms towards the west, and its lower extremities (the author in the Latin language uses words more particular) towards the east. The Steeple represents the head, with an enormous neck, rising upwards of eighteen stories into the clouds, and surrounded with two battlements, or galleries – one in the middle, and another at the top, like a crown adorning the head; whose loud-sounding tongue daily calls the people to worship.

'The right hand is stretched forth to the poor, for there is a large and well-furnished hospital on this side; but the left hand, because nearer the heart, is more elevated towards heaven than the right, indicating a devout mind panting after celestial joys. In the inmost recesses of the breath stand the sacred temples of God. So remarkable were the people of this place for their adherence to true religion, that, at the Reformation, it was honoured with the appellation of "the second Geneva".

'On the left breast is a Christian burial-place, richly and piously ornamented, that the pious dead may be long held in admiration and esteem. On the belly is the market-place, at the middle of which is the cross...'

(translated from the Latin of the Reverend Robert Edward of Murroes [1678] in *Dundee Delineated; or, A History and Description of that Town* [1822])

Executive Quatrains/Captain My Captain (125)
The italicised sections of these poems are ekphrastic responses to an exhibition of paintings by Don Van Vliet (Captain Beefheart) held in the Waddington Gallery, in Cork Street, London, 3-26 April 1986. Specific paintings are referred to as follows:
'Language you were always going to tell us': *Red Shell Bats* and *Aunt Cigar's Baby*
'What is it like this to imagine someone': *See Through Dog with Wheat Stack Skirt*
'To listen as ekphrasis is an act of praise': *Tidle Wholder*

'The high desert for your ocean floor': *Green Tom*
'You knew from the inside of childhood': *Black Kang Nail* and *Ballerina Weiner*
'The mess of ages has got into the messages': *Apalucha* and *Night Print*
'Caged in renegado cabin': *Fur on the Trellis* and *Just Up into the Air, Scratch of Light*, and *Dylisheus*
'The great moment keeps passing': *When I See Mommy I Feel Like a Mummy* and *Measures Balance*

Kirsty Wark on Broughty Ferry Beach (187)
Kirsty Wark is a Scottish presenter on the BBC2 flagship news prog-ramme, *Newsnight*. The Phibbie Pier is the Broughty Ferry pier where the Ancient Association of Amphibians (a river swimming club) meet. Cox and Marra are the actor Brian Cox, and the son of the singer Michael Marra; while 'aa ae oo' means all woven from a single threud.

Bad Makar McGonagalliana (194)
Mary Shelley visited Dundee as an adolescent, staying with the Baxters, a rich family of linen manufacturers from 1812 to 1814. Kengo Kuma is a 'zenimalist' architect, who designed the Dundee V&A. James Cameron was a prominent journalist who worked for Dundee firm D.C. Thomson's before the Second World War. The samurai Miyamoto Musashi, author of *The Book of the Five Rings*, is depicted in a fantastic print by Utigawa Kuniyoshi killing a right whale with his sword 'off the coast of Hizen'. The *Physiologus* is a didactic account of the appearance and behaviour of animals, not all of which are found in nature. It dates from the 2nd century AD, and was widely copied and translated. While there is no *Logie Physiologus*, the early 13th-century *Aberdeen Bestiary* gives some indication of how such a manu-script might have looked. The Jif Lemon Tree was located beside the Tay Road Bridge, not far from the site of the V&A, and was a tree hung with plastic lemons by toll collectors working on the bridge. Dei Donum (God's gift) is a false etymology for the origin of the name 'Dundee', supposedly given by the Earl of Huntingdon for reaching harbour in a storm on his return from the Crusades. It is one of two mottoes on the city crest.

The Couthier (203)
The Courier and Advertiser is one of a number of newspapers and magazines published by D.C. Thomson's, among which are the formerly-radical *People's Friend*, the now-defunct *Sporting Post*, and the still-extant *Evening Telegraph* or *'Tully'*. The 'Craigie Column', like *The People's Friend*, mostly focusses on nostalgic reminiscence,

while 'Dixon Hawke' and 'Bill & Ben' were long-running series, the first a detective, and the second a cartoon which, like Rupert the Bear, delivered its text in verse.

Undeed (204)

The Eternity stone was laid in St Peter's churchyard in commemoration of Robert Annan, a lay evangelical preacher also known as the Water Dog, who concluded his final sermon by chalking 'Eternity' on the pavement, and asking 'Where will you spend Eternity?' (The incident ascribed to my father in Kidderpore docks in 'Wreck of the *Javanese Princess*' (56) was originally supposed to have happened to Annan while in America.)

Mastercannibal (206)

'A little to the west of the farmhouse of Denfind, formerly Dunfind, there is a deep ravine called Denfiend, through which a rivulet runs... In Lindsay of Pitscottie's History... it is called the Fiend's Den, because a brigand with his family dwelt in it. 'He had an execrable fashion to all young men and children that he could steal or obtain by other means, and take them home and eat them... For these acts he was burned with his wife, bairns, and family, except a young lass of one year old, who was saved and taken to Dundee, where she was brought up, but when she came to women's years, she was condemned and burned quick for the same crime her father and mother were convicted of. A great crowd, chiefly women, attended at the execution, cursing her for her crimes. To them she said – "Why chide ye me as if I had committed a crime. Give me credit, if ye had the experience of eating human flesh you would think it so delicious that you would never forbear it again."' (*Angus or Forfarshire* by A.J. Warden, quoting Lindsay of Pitscottie's *Historie and Cronicles of Scotland*, 1884)